CHANGING WORLDS SERIES

I0101308

Davos and the
GREAT RESET

APMI Publications
a division of Alan Pateman Ministries
Tuscany, Italy

By Dr. Alan Pateman

By Dr. Jennifer Pateman

AVAILABLE FROM APMI PUBLICATIONS, AMAZON.COM AND OTHER RETAIL OUTLETS

CHANGING WORLDS SERIES

DR. ALAN PATEMAN

Apocalypse, endtimes,
the end has begun

Davos and the
GREAT RESET

❖

BOOK 2 OF A 3 BOOK
CHANGING WORLDS SERIES

BOOK TITLE:
Davos and the Great Reset

This edition published in 2023

Published by APMI Publications
In Partnership with Truth for the Journey Books **40**
P.O. Box 17,
55051 Barga (LU),
Italy

Email: publications@alanpateman.com
www.watchersofthe4kings.com/apmi-publishing
www.facebook.com/Watchersofthe4Kings

APMI Publications and Truth for the Journey Books are a division of Alan Pateman Ministries

Printed in the United States of America, Europe and Asia

Paperback ISBN: 978-1-909132-26-9
eBook ISBN: 978-1-909132-27-6

Acknowledgements:
Author/Design/Senior Editor/Publisher: Apostle Dr. Alan Pateman
Editing/Proofreading/Research: Dr. Jennifer Pateman
Computer Administration/Office Manager: Dr. Dorothea Struhlik
Cover Image Credit: www.PosterMyWall.com

❖

Dedication

I would like to dedicate this book to
Leearna and Danny Pilgram.
Thank you for your love and partnership.

❖

Table of Contents

❖

Introduction

This book, **"Davos and the Great Reset"** *(which is the second book of a three book series, called Changing Worlds)* is not meant to be a fact finding analytical mission of compounded research, but is more prophetic in nature. An overview of what's happening in the world and on the political scene – and what it means to the Church in these unbelievable times. You might say it's a conversation!

Have you heard the latest chatter about the new version of the famous and long talked about, **New World Order?** It has a new slogan called the **"Great Reset."** Everyone from the Canadian Prime Minister Justin Trudeau, to the Italian Pope Francis, to the British Charles the Royal Prince of Wales *(who is now the King of England)* are enthusiastically touting this new globalist catchphrase, "Build Back Better."

Watching them fawn over themselves with glee, we mustn't fail to recognize that "COVID-19 Pandemic" was not a hoax, it was real and has affected many lives. Yet, it's no coincidence that it has simultaneously presented these globalists with a seemingly perfectly calculated **"opportunity"** to usher in a whole new global order.

When we talk like this, we sound so conspiratorial and when they talk, they sound like the adult in the room, so noble and so caring of society and nature! Really?

Yes, the Great Reset sounds like just another conspiracy theory, *(to add to an ever-growing list).* However when the bible states that even the elect can be deceived, who can afford to be cavalier about the future? AND if we reduce everything to a conspiracy, don't we run the risk of joining the global herd that's willing to believe whatever the MS *(mainstream media)* and their governments tell them to believe!

POLLYANNA MIND SET

It's never that simple and as believers we can't afford to have a naïve Pollyanna mind-set that accepts everything as fate or good-karma, especially when it comes to politics. Kumbaya prayer meetings won't cut it either. Though we are faith people, we must also be realists, who recognize that not everything is going to be ok, chiefly if the wrong people seize power.

Scripture fuels true intercession, it is not misguided. As the following verse shows, peace is only ever the result of righteousness, which must be legislated from the top down:

When the righteous are in authority, the people rejoice: but when the wicked beareth rule, the people mourn.

(Proverbs 29:2 KJV)

Sophisticated elite types, consider everyone else beside themselves, *primitive*. Yet their policies always seem to produce division, negativity and dystopian darkness:

*This wisdom descendeth not from above, but is earthly, sensual, devilish. For where envying and strife is, **there is confusion and every evil work.***

(James 3:15-16 KJV)

The make-believe world of utopia always produces hell, always. Every utopian movement has produced hell on earth.

—Dennis Prayer of PragerU[1]

So unless righteous people take their place, other more unrighteous entities will fill every available vacuum of power: ***"From the days of John the Baptist until now the kingdom of heaven suffers violent assault, and violent men seize it by force as a precious prize"*** *(Matthew 11:12 AMP)*.

Ultimately, we know what the angel said to Mary concerning Jesus that day: ***"He will reign over the house of Jacob (Israel) forever, and of His kingdom there shall be no end"*** *(Luke 1:33 AMP)*.

CURRENT POLITICAL AFFAIRS

However, in current political affairs, tyranny relies on our inertia. I emphasize once more, while advocating for the

Good News, we mustn't turn our backs on reality. Battles are raging all around us in order to stop righteousness growing its influence and to remove every obstacle from their global agenda.

Consider various biblical figures such as Joseph, Daniel and Nehemiah, who were all involved in the politics of their day. Whether through Pharaohs or Kings, they came face to face with despots of tyranny. Yet look how God used them, all while facing overwhelming backlash and resistance from every side.

We are to test every spirit the bible instructs. Does this include the spirit behind our policy makers? Who is pulling their strings exactly? What do their policies stand for - before we blindly co-sign with something diabolical like the slaughter of children known as infanticide? Considering our children and their future world experience, we better get woke!

BEING WOKE TODAY

Incidentally there's much talk of being *"woke"* today, specifically by the media who use it *ad-nauseam*. But who decides who's *woke* or not? Every social justice warrior out there thinks they're more woke than the next person, when little do they realise just how *unseeing* they truly are, as they continue to parrot ideas that have been purposefully fed to them.

Conflicting definitions exist on the subject of being "woke" which is chiefly an American slang term for being:

"Aware of and actively attentive to important facts and issues *(especially issues of racial and social justice)."* Others suggest that it's, "The act of being very *pretentious* about how much you care about a social issue"! **Either way, if you're going to be woke about *anything*, let it be TRUTH.**[2]

PROBLEM-SOLVE ON A GLOBAL SCALE

Those who meet every year in Davos, Switzerland are planning for *our* future, to the point that we will own nothing *(that part always gets people to pay attention).* Now, I have written much on Marxist ideas and the confiscation of property, which is nothing new. Remember chapter 10 of the book of Hebrews, which discusses sacrifice, and the perseverance of faith:

> *You joyfully accepted* **the [unjust] seizure of your belongings and the confiscation of your property,** *conscious of the fact that you have a better possession and a lasting one prepared for you in heaven.*
> (Hebrews 10:34 AMP)

The seizure of property is of course unjust, along with the restriction of movements. There'll come a point in time, that in order to travel, one will require permission. Consider that! Still, elites work hard to convince us that we will feel safer, happier and stronger for it!

The Great Reset is actually nothing new. It has been talked about openly for some time now and introduced openly at the World Economic Forum (WEF) in Davos Switzerland, where the world's most powerful people gather to *problem-solve* on a global scale.

In fact footage is readily available from Davos 2019 where the founders enthusiastically rolled out this said "Reset."

———————————

ENDNOTES:

1. FiresideChat Ep.163 - "Is Capitalism Evil?" https://www.prageru. com/video/ep-163-is-capitalism-evil/ Dennis Prager of PragerU video produced Dec 03, 2020. Accessed via YouTube 11.12.20

2. https://www.merriam-webster.com/dictionary/woke https://www.urbandictionary.com/define.php?term=woke Dictionary definition of WOKE accessed 11/12/20

3. Scripture quotations marked AMP are taken from the Amplified® Bible, Copyright © 2015 by The Lockman Foundation. Used by permission. (www.Lockman.org)

4. Scripture quotations marked KJV are taken from the King James Version of the Bible.

❖

CHAPTER 1

Big Tech & The Technocrats

CENSORSHIP & SECTION 230

Hopefully you would have read my first book of this series, *"The Great Reset Deception"* as it's impossible to confine so much information that needs to be brought to light, just in one book.

Remember, "The great reset is a means to an end. Next on the agenda is a complete makeover of society under a technocratic regime of un-elected bureaucrats *(World Economic Forum, WEF, in Davos Switzerland)* who want to dictate how the world is run from the top down, leveraging invasive technologies to track and trace your every move while censoring and silencing anyone who dares not comply."[1]

However in this chapter we will start with the implications of media and the influence that it has in changing our society.

ADDRESSING BIG TECH

YouTube recently announced that it would remove all content that alleges widespread election fraud and the conversation about Big Tech's abuses of power have gotten much louder! Currently there is a battle waging over the need for legislation to deal once and for all with "Section 230" of the Communications Decency Act, US *(currently shielding the likes of Twitter, Facebook, Google and YouTube from liability).*

> **Big Tech censorship is the single greatest threat to democracy...**
>
> — Ted Cruz

One staunch advocate for the removal of "Section 230" is U.S. Sen. Ted Cruz who says, "Silicon Valley believes there is no power on Earth that can constrain them. We saw the latest illustration of this just yesterday *(at the time of writing this book),* where YouTube announced that it is going to remove any content online that alleges widespread election fraud. YouTube said that it's going to pull down, it's going to block, content, 'that misleads people by alleging widespread fraud or errors change the outcome of the presidential election.' They're not even pretending anymore."

When asked about the abuses of Section 230 and the lack of accountability by Big Tech, Mark Zuckerberg said the following:

Section 230 made it possible for every major internet service to be built and ensured important values like free expression and openness were part of how platforms operate.

— Mark Zuckerberg[2]

I wonder what he means exactly by "free expression" and who it's intended for! Because the new motto of the left has become increasingly evident, *"free speech for me, but not for thee!"*

Cruz stated: "I am not asking you to pull down liberal content. I'm not asking you to pull down socialists. I'm not asking you to pull down communists. **I disagree with liberal content and socialists and communists, but I believe in free speech.** It is only one side that is demanding of Big Tech that they censor the views they disagree with."

The argument centers on this element, that Big Tech is political. It leans one way and is censoring its political opponents while pretending to be advocates for free speech. Big Tech seemingly wants to pull all the strings and have total control of public debate. Silicon Valley billionaires have wealth and power but zero accountability. Most importantly, *"... they're not elected by anyone."*

They run companies the size of small countries, with vast resources, that exceed the GDP of many small countries! They hold enormous sway and influence. The danger is this, if the government controls the Internet, then there is zero freedom of speech. Equally so, internet monopolies must be broken up, because they get too big and to controlling, when they not just "corner the market" but literally own it, they can bully the world.

ADDRESSING MONOPOLY

Addressing monopoly, Cruz went on, "The purpose [Section 230] served when these were nascent companies has long since passed, **these are the most powerful companies on the face of the Earth and they feel zero accountability to any elected official.**

For all of us who care about free speech, that should worry us greatly. YouTube's latest policy is ridiculous. And by the way, if they disagree with someone saying there's widespread election fraud, there's a mechanism for that, which is they can share their own views. You can counter it, you can say, I think this is all baloney. That's fine. That's called free speech, but simply exercising monopoly power to say the views that I don't like shall disappear and have never existed, that should scare everyone."

Reuters polling shows that 39 percent of the American people believe that the 2020 election was rigged…
— Ted Cruz[3]

BECOMING A GLOBE OF SNITCHES!

I have to congratulate some writers for their articles during COVID because I like common sense writing.

Jen Gerson wrote an opinion piece back in April 2020, in Maclean's, *(which claims to be Canada's premier current affairs magazine)*. She states, **"Don't let coronavirus turn us into a**

nation of snitches. Hotlines for reporting 'non-compliance' are evil tools that will damage the very trust we'll need to rebound from this crisis.

Social media has become a difficult place for me, of late… Take, for example, the Twitter hash tag trend #Covidiots: initially intended to accompany candid camera shots of callous young people gathering, it grew into a broader habit of gleefully shaming anybody displaying behaviours that were considered sane and normal only a few weeks ago.

I struggle to share in the schadenfreude — or ritual humiliation, or whatever you care to call it — despite the sudden consensus that this was the new, patriotic thing to do…

Certainly, there has been willful flouting of common sense restrictions… The term #Covidiots is not always unwarranted. Both informed and consenting citizens will continue to engage in social distancing to the degree to which they are able; or we are going to accept increasingly authoritarian measures of social control…

THE SNITCH LINES

But of all these developments, there is nothing that I find more disturbing than the snitch lines. Right across the country, provinces and municipalities have established hotlines to report social distancing failures.

Snitching may work, but the downsides to citizen-policing are grim — to say nothing of the historical antecedents. Totalitarian states turned neighbour against neighbour and family against family, in order to maintain the illusion of social cohesion.

Authoritarians use this tactic because there are never enough police or soldiers to force compliance upon an entire population, not unless everyone consents to become an agent of his or her own mutual oppression.

The term 'fascism' has an innocent history. It comes from the Roman term 'fasces,' which means a bundle of sticks bound together. One stick breaks, but the fasces remains strong. It's another term for unity. That's what makes it so seductive, especially in times of uncertainty and mortal dread. We're all in this together. Nary a stick shall stray.

'We are now living amid the very tactics that the West [once] criticized,' Polsky added. 'With state controls on commerce, industry, speech, and media.'

'Extraordinary times require extraordinary measures and it is about protecting the public,' Privy Council President Dominic LeBlanc told reporters with a line that should give any student of history the creeps.

No doubt LeBlanc et al are operating under the noblest of intentions. But repressive measures buy conformity at a terrible price. Snitch lines turn us against one another. **They teach us to fear the people we need to survive, thus making us more dependent on the apparatus of the state.**

Snitch lines are an evil tool in a time of crisis because they damage the trust that we need to create resiliency in our communities. I would encourage you to think really hard before reporting on the neighbour for playing ball with his daughter in the park, or lingering too long in a parking lot, or sitting too close on a bench.

**This pandemic will pass.
Our fear will pass. What will remain?
Is what we've allowed ourselves to become."[4]**

Then another opinion piece appeared in the NY Times in August, entitled:

Don't Make College Kids the Coronavirus Police.

"Many universities are asking students to wear masks and avoid parties — and to report on peers who break the rules. It could backfire."[5]

———————

ENDNOTES:

1. By Tim Hinchliffe of The Sociable. https://sociable.co/government-and-policy/timeline-great-reset-agenda-event-201-pandemic-2020/

2. https://www.businessinsider.com/congress-section-230-repeal-crush-social-media-facebook-twitter-google-2020-10?IR=T

3. December 11, 2020 - https://www.cruz.senate.gov/?p=press_release&id=5512. Accessed 15.12.20

4. https://www.macleans.ca/opinion/dont-let-coronavirus-turn-us-into-a-nation-of-snitches/ Maclean's is Canada's premier current affairs magazine. By Jen Gerson. April 20, 2020

5. By Karen Levy and Lauren Kilgour. Aug. 12, 2020 - https://www.nytimes.com/2020/08/12/opinion/coronavirus-college-reopening.html

❖

CHAPTER 2

Year 2020 was Most Unusual

5 AREAS OF CHANGE TO WATCH OUT FOR!

It started with an unprecedented global pandemic caused by the CCP virus, and it concluded with the U.S. presidential election, which captivated the world.

1. Abolishing the Norm:

On election night, on Nov. 3, an assortment of anomalies were observed, followed by a large number of specific allegations of election fraud. As the integrity of the election continued to be questioned and evidence continued to emerge, most mainstream media stuck to a one-sided narrative by calling the 2020 election the most secure in American history, and sought to silence opposing voices.

The results of the 2020 election will not only decide the future of the United States, but also determine the future of the world.[1]

2. The Tyrannical takeover of the Individual:

Tyranny abolishes every concept of *individuality*, where the individual no longer exists. Any ideas of personal ownership, preference, choice or lifestyle are made obsolete. Instead everything must be monitored and routine, including diet. When our governments dictate the food we eat, this becomes a strong indicator that we're no longer free to make any meaningful decisions of our own.

Individualism is meaningless in a totalitarian society. BUT as part of a whole unit, we're supposed to feel safer, stronger, healthier and happier as a result. Don't forget that!

3. The Currency Manipulator:

All personal monies will ultimately be confiscated. Until then, consider that digital money is much easier to control than cash.

> **Side note:** *My wife and I generally give to beggars in our local town, but there are days when we have no cash because we've used credit cards to shop with.*

In a cashless society, how will they survive? Yet socialism claims to eradicate homelessness because everyone will have the *"same"* opportunities. Everything will be *"equal"* and *"shared."* I wonder how Venezuela feels about that concept!

Nevertheless, the reality of a cashless society is just a hop-skip-and-a-jump away and once our personal recourses are fully controlled, so will we be. There won't be much freedom at that point. Private equity, homes, cars, family savings and inheritance will all be confiscated and belong to those in control at the top of the pyramid. Yet they'll continue to advance the notion that it's in our best interest, for welfare and safety etc., etc. (*…you get my point*)

> *Side Note: Sites like the New Socialist want to put a new modern socialistic twist on private equity. Perhaps take a look and judge for yourselves. It all sounds so very noble indeed!*[2]

4. Population Control:

Such a scenario of complete population control simply makes the "Left" giddy, personally I don't share the excitement of such Communist philosophy that argues against private property and supports collective ownership, and where even our ideas are not our own.

I just read an article today: Public Goods and Intellectual Property Rights, on a website concerning Communism and Computer Ethics; it stated in its very opening:

> Communist philosophy argues against private property and supports collective ownership. This philosophy applies specifically to intellectual property and software. The common view is that no person should own or control any property, whether electronic, merely an idea, or otherwise.[3]

5. Fact Not Fiction:

Don't be fooled into supposing that all this is just in the realm of conspiracy theory. I know the likes of Alex Jones and InfoWars have repelled and freaked people out for decades. However, when it comes to these elites at Davos, they're hiding their ideas for *world domination* - in plain sight – we just need to be paying attention!

Safe are they, if we think it's just another conspiracy! Because one day we will wake up and realise they were "dead serious" about their ambitions to alter the entire way our current world operates.

As seen recently on CBN World News, one leading authority on this particular subject is Justin Haskins, who has said openly:

"This is not a conspiracy theory. This is a well-documented movement among many of the world's most powerful people... Fundamentally, this is a radical and complete transformation of everything that we do in our society... It will change the way businesses are evaluated, it will coerce businesses to pursue left-wing causes."[4]

———————

ENDNOTES:

1. Whose Stealing America? by Joshua Phillips. https://www.theepochtimes.com/2020-election-investigation-who-is-stealing-america_3617562.html; https://www.patreon.com/posts/45031044; https://www.theepochtimes.com

2. https://newsocialist.org.uk/private-equity-and-people/

3. Site was accessed 11.12.20. https://cs.stanford.edu/people/eroberts/cs201/projects/communism-computing-china/intelproperty.html

4. https://www1.cbn.com/cbnnews/world/2020/december/the-great-reset; Written by Dale Hurd on 08-12-2020. Site was accessed 10/12/20

❖

CHAPTER 3

Environment of
Mass Misinformation

WIDELY READ AND WELL INFORMED

I have to emphasise, although it should go without saying, it's vital that we, especially as believers, are widely read and well informed.

Asking questions like: *"How does our faith play-out in a world like this?"* We must choose very carefully our sources of information, especially in this global environment of *mass-misinformation*.

Let's endeavour to quote directly from experts and scholars who are widely known and recognized, as authorities in their field.

33

On the *Great Reset,* **Justin Haskins** is a solid source of accurate information. Some of his accolades include the fact that he's currently the executive editor and a research fellow at the **"Heartland Institute"** and the editor-in-chief of "StoppingSocialism.com" as well as author of **"Socialism Is Evil: The Moral Case Against Marx's Radical Dream."**

Additionally Justin's an Opinion Contributor for The Hill and recently wrote the following excerpt:

A GREAT RESET OF CAPITALISM

"In June, elites at important international institutions such as the World Economic Forum and the United Nations launched a far-reaching campaign to *'reset'* the global economy. The plan involves dramatically increasing the power of government through expansive new social programs like the *Green New Deal* and using vast regulatory schemes and government programs to coerce corporations into supporting left-wing causes.

The two justifications for the proposal, which has been aptly named by its supporters the *'Great Reset,'* are the COVID-19 pandemic *(the short-term justification)* and the so-called 'climate crisis' caused by global warming *(the long-term justification).*

According to the Great Reset's supporters, the plan would fundamentally transform much of society. As World Economic Forum (WEF) head **Klaus Schwab** wrote back in June,

The world must act jointly and swiftly to revamp all aspects of our societies and economies, from education to social contracts and working conditions. Every country, from the United States to China, must participate, and every industry, from oil and gas to tech, must be transformed. **In short, we need a 'Great Reset' of capitalism.**

Internationally, influential leaders, activists, academics and institutions have already backed the Great Reset. In addition to the World Economic Forum and United Nations, the Great Reset movement counts among its [supporters] *(sic)* the International Monetary Fund, heads of state, Greenpeace and CEOs and presidents of large corporations and financial institutions such as Microsoft and MasterCard.

But in America, most policymakers – including President Joe Biden have been relatively quiet about the *Great Reset*, leaving many to speculate what a Biden administration would do to support or oppose this radical plan.

There has been some evidence suggesting that Biden and some of his biggest allies back the *Great Reset* and would attempt to impose it on the United States. But Biden and his team have never explicitly stated that America would be involved — *that is, until now.*

At a panel discussion about the *Great Reset* hosted by the World Economic Forum in mid-November, former Secretary of State John Kerry, Biden's would-be - *special presidential envoy for climate* - firmly declared that the Biden administration will support the *Great Reset* and that the *Great Reset 'will happen with greater speed and with greater intensity than a lot of people might imagine.'"*[1]

Perhaps you feel the same way that I do, *(not that I am looking for an echo chamber)*; that this entire "global opportunity" [COVID-19] has conveniently made way for a carefully crafted plan to take over the world. *"They"* needed something to accelerate their vision of global-socialism, whether we like it or not.

In addition, one cannot fail to perceive, that with a *hand-in-glove-type-synergy* the Big-Tec companies and social media giants have been utterly complicit and overly accommodating this said RESET. Even now as they ramp up their censorship of all opposing ideas that question their agenda, *(not least conservative thought)*.

RE-EDUCATION CAMPS

I don't want to digress too far down this particular rabbit hole, but it is relevant. There is much talk online at present and has been for some time now about *"re-education camps"* for conservatives or so called *"right-wingers."*

It's a terrifying reality and proves that our universities have been breeding a hot bed of trained Marxist thinkers, who are now able, ready and willing to embrace and perhaps *enforce* a whole new world. Tossing away their freedom as if it meant nothing. What you feed, breeds. It appears they don't consider any parallels with former Nazi Germany or the likes of what China is doing to re-educate Muslims and other minority groups, even as we speak.

Folks, this is real, it's dangerous and gaining momentum. Let me quote what I saw on *reddit.com* just this morning over coffee; it'll help solidify my point. In keeping it brief, I'll also keep the random usernames anonymous, yet quote them directly.

Arguing in favour of "re-education camps" - Reddit.com:

Anonymous user No.1:
Someone posted a meme about how every right-winger should be put in re-education camps. When I pointed out that political opponents were the first people put in Nazi concentration camps, I got hit with **"Yeah but they were Nazis, we're not!"**

Anonymous user No.2:
Yea it's a fun time to live in when people can't draw parallels to previous times.

Anonymous user No.3:
I'd be happy if they just went to education camps.

Anonymous user No.4:
Only if they're openly resisting the new order. I know it sounds bad but if the day ever comes and we overthrow capitalism then **it's not just the billionaires who'll have to be executed, a lot of your average right-wingers will have to be as well.**

Anonymous user No.5:
One day we will have super intelligent computers solving extremely complex social and economic problems for us. We will increasingly depend on this technology to help us define our own policies. I don't expect that our AI oracles will confirm that right-

wingers need to be put into camps. **But I do think it is inevitable that AI will identify right wing ideology as a threat to civilization and prioritize this as a problem that needs to be fixed if we want to survive.**[2]

This is chilling indeed and it would be a race-to-the-bottom if these folks were in charge. Nevertheless this represents a tiny drop in the ocean, of web chatter and activity on this subject. Many have been sold on the idea that the world would be a better place if it were purged of "right-wingers" *(the ultimate scourge on humanity!)* Sadly this type of thinking happens when the Church fails to influence society and allows Communist Marxism to instead.

GLOBAL SOCIALISM

Global socialism is the elite's vision of a final solution to the global Pandemic COVID-19, *(and by contrived coincidence it had to be socialism!)* According to some, since the great purge of 2020's global pandemic, the world can now be a better place, *(actually it was the shut-downs that purged us).* They say we can, "BUILD BACK BETTER." I urge you to watch closely who actually uses this slogan, it's revealing. Who knew that Pope Francis was a Left-leaning socialist? *(I jest not).*

So far we've had shut downs that make no sense, and have quarantined the healthy with the sick. Now people are dying of suicide and other untreated illnesses, due to restrictions from COVID-19. For example some with cancer did not keep their chemo appointments, because they feared Covid-19 more.

Then there is the homelessness problem and many other maladies now plaguing society, the numbers are above and beyond those impacted by the pandemic. In fact, most were NOT impacted by the disease, rather the shutdown.

It's now widely recognised how the solution has proved worse than the problem. I'll spare you the numbers, though any average "Jack" on the streets *(minus some fancy degrees but loaded with plain-old-common-sense)* could see that the shutdowns were utterly unsustainable.

POWERING THE GREAT RESET

Those in Geneva at the World Economic Forum believe we don't need God to build back better, we can do it ourselves. We don't need deity, we are self-sufficient and we are smart enough. We are the gods of the future and there is nothing we cannot do if we put our minds and efforts together.

> *"We are the future - God is the past. God scattered them then… he can scatter them now! Is it time for another global scattering?"*

I stumbled across this site about the WEF - though I wasn't looking for it *(the Holy Spirit leads our research I'm telling you).*

Digital Transformation Powering the Great Reset JULY 2020:

This reset has long been masterminded and not just a convenient occurrence due to Covid-19. It's the infrastructure of a New World Order that is very organized.

World Economic Forum

- "COVID-19 has irrevocably changed our world."
  "Reimagining digital transformation"
  The rising urgency of digital transformation
  The digital dividend is gigantic...
  Time to shift gears: add purpose to digital transformation

- **Three opportunities for corporate leadership:**

  Opportunity 1: Transform business
  Digital transformation and the seven dimensions in the new normal:
  Seven dimensions
  Principles to guide the digital transformation journey

  Opportunity 2: Empower stakeholders

  Opportunity 3: Change systems
  Accelerating digital transformation
  "The World Economic Forum, committed to improving the state of the world, is the International Organization for Public-Private Cooperation.
  The Forum engages the foremost political, business and other leaders of society to shape global, regional and industry agendas."[3]

It looks massive but we overcome the world by faith *(Hebrews 11:1)* and the great scattering will come... elites don't own God. They don't have a monopoly on the world. *(Now I know why I loathed that game so much, whilst growing up!)*

It's too much to talk about, it blows my brain and I thought I could handle a lot! But I've given headlines only.

An investigative journalist like Joshua Phillips *(I highly recommend The Epoch Times)* would analyse the data with a microscope but we are just having a conversation.

It can make you feel like an ant from the Ant Movie my kids used to watch - narrated by Woody Allen. His character said to his therapist, *"I feel irrelevant"* and his therapist said, *"Good. You've made excellent progress."* He replies, *"I have?"* *"Yes! Because you ARE irrelevant!"*

In the face of it all, the size of it all - makes one feel puny - but our God is so large. He will never be irrelevant, scripture declares Him in Psalm 121:1 the maker of heavens and the earth… what could ever be irrelevant about that!

Is Artificial Intelligence (AI) the Antichrist?

Yes, because anything that is against Christ is anti-Christ. It views us as a public menace, who need to be reformed and reeducated and that our belief system needs to be reimagined and reengineered to exclude Judeo-Christian values.

What about the Gregorian calendar?
Will that go too in this purge?
Is this now a completely pagan world system?
[As the Gregorian calendar is based on the pope and Catholic Church].

It's too big, but God it's not too big for you. It's easy to call everyone else cowards. Up in the stands at a far distance. Behind a screen or a book. Opinions don't matter, actions do.

Fans that can't control a ball to save their lives, often berate tennis players and football players during a game as if they were pros themselves (delusion!)

Likewise, we can't be keyboard (pseudo) warriors... Jesus make us real warriors, not so spiritual that we are zero earthly good.

ENDNOTES:

1. https://thehill.com/opinion/energy-environment/528482-john-kerry-reveals-bidens-devotion-to-radical-great-reset-movement; Excerpt in The Hill was written by Justin Haskins, the Editorial Director at The Heartland Institute. And a leading authority on the Great Reset - 12/03/20 11:30 - AM EST. Accessed the site 10.12.20. Also editor-in-chief of StoppingSocialism.com. Also author of "Socialism Is Evil: The Moral Case Against Marx's Radical Dream."

2. https://www.reddit.com/r/insanepeoplefacebook/comments/fz5ygc/arguing_in_favor_of_reeducation_camps_for/; https://www.reddit.com/r/insanepeoplefacebook/

3. World Economic Forum; 91–93 route de la Capite CH-1223 Cologny/Geneva Switzerland. Tel.: +41 (0) 22 869 1212 Fax: +41 (0) 22 786 2744 contact@weforum.org www.weforum.org; http://www3.weforum.org/docs/WEF_Digital_Transformation_Powering_the_Great_Reset_2020.pdf

❖

CHAPTER 4

2020 Election and the Church

A UNIQUE TIME

In this chapter, which explores the link between the Church and the 2020 US election, I first want to interject the importance of speaking from a Christian viewpoint, especially when writing a book about Davos and the Great Reset, which is essentially atheistic and anti-Christian at its core.

The global consequence of this is that the Christian worldview, which is more aligned with and represented by conservatives — the right of the political spectrum — which is coming increasingly under attack.

Let's begin then by saying by early 2021 everyone was mad at the prophets who were on TV doing damage control.

There were many of them who were fast to make predictions, and seemed to be jumping on the political bandwagon, caught up in the hype of the rallies surrounding the election on November 3rd 2020. A unique time for sure. But I will mention prophecy, just briefly because it was all part of the journey. Were they right or wrong? Let's not be so swift to condemn. Time will reveal all things.

Shortly after the US Presidential election, polls emerged revealing the shifting sentiments and stark division. According to an article by Catherine Kim from Politico, who said,

> After the presidential race was called for Democratic candidate Joe Biden, Republicans' trust in the election system plummeted, while Democrats' trust soared... 70 percent of Republicans now say they don't believe the 2020 election was free and fair... Ninety percent of Democrats now say the election was free and fair...[1]

DOES THIS SIGNAL CIVIL WAR?

So does this signal civil war? Irrespective of who wins or who loses, at this point both sides are so deeply entrenched and divided that chaos is likely to ensue regardless. Remember how everything was boarded up in DC just prior to the elections? Yet all those protests and displays of anarchy that had plagued the entire summer - in states like Portland *(Oregon)*, Seattle *(Washington)* and others - suddenly halted after the election. What does this tell us?

Whether it was the George Floyd protests against systemic racism, Antifa, BLM *(Black Lives Matter)*, the call to defund the Police, etc., the violence was stoked like fire. Was this really orchestrated and coordinated violence? It certainly looked that way. In fact all that violence seemed to take a back seat and instant breather after the election. Nevertheless it felt like the calm-before-the-storm with everything hinging on the results of the election.

PROPHETIC PREDICTIONS 2020

The bible warns us, "do not treat prophecies with contempt…" and that God "does nothing without revealing his plan to his servants the prophets…" *(1 Thessalonians 5:19; Amos 3:7)* So it's not time to scoff.

Just prior to the election, Pat Robertson made some very bold predictions. *(See endnote for YouTube link).* However, it's not just Pat, it's many of the recognised prophets, that came out in the same way. AND when all the prophets are saying the same thing, it's time to pay attention.

When they're all prophesying that Trump will get back in for a second term, either a spirit of gross error and delusion has deceived all of them "at once" which is unlikely, or they're right! Let's see.

At this point, it's as if the false prophets of Baal are shouting, jeering and mocking from one side of the mountain *(the main stream media),* at God's prophets who are all on the other side *(light vs. dark).*

Pat's Prophetic Prediction as Follows:

1. Trump will win the election and get in for a second term

2. Civic unrest will ensue
3. There'll be at least 2 attempts on the President's life
4. The country will be torn apart
5. War against Israel
6. God will intervene supernaturally
7. A Revival and period of great peace take over for about 5 years
8. Followed by a period of great tribulation that will occur suddenly
9. Culminating in the return of Christ *(perhaps)*

Pat starts off by stating that he believes Trump will get in for a second term. That he will be sworn in, and then the chaos will begin! Predicting challenges from China, North Korea and Turkey that will come.

GREAT CIVIL DISCORD

For America however he predicts great civil discord and that the country will be torn apart. Beyond that, there will be **"at least" two attempts on the president's life and how the time following will be very difficult indeed.**

Therefore, son of man, prophesy and say to Gog: "This is what the Sovereign LORD says: In that day, when my people Israel are living in safety, will you not take notice of it? You will come from your place in the far north, you and many nations with you, all of them riding on horses, a **great horde, a mighty army.** *You will advance against my people Israel like a cloud that covers the land. In days to come, Gog, I will bring you against my land, so that the* *nations may know me when I am proved holy through you before their eyes."*

(Ezekiel 38:14-16)

A TREMENDOUS HORDE

Pat goes on to say that this would present an *"opportunity"* for the likes of Turkey and Iran especially, to come up against Israel, as it says in Ezekiel above. A tremendous *"horde"* consisting of elements from parts of Russia, Iran, Yemen and even North Sudan *(representing all those who hate Israel),* and that they will form a *"coalition"* that will come together.

This coalition will take advantage of the fact that America is so preoccupied in order to invade Israel but God will defend Israel supernaturally. *"It's NOT going to be nuclear,"* Pat said, *"But God Himself is going to wipe out that horde of people coming against Israel."*

Then Pat predicts a remarkable time of PEACE *(Isaiah 2:2-4),* lasting approximately five years, a time when world dictators and aggressors *(who want war)* will be restrained. During which time there will be a global revival like the world has never seen before – a great turning to God.

After enjoying such peace, there will come a period of great tribulation:

The Lord will come like a thief in the night. While people are saying, **"Peace and safety,"** *destruction will* **come on them suddenly,** *as labour pains on a pregnant woman, and they will not escape.*

(1 Thessalonians 5:2-3)

In Jesus's own words He warns,

> For then there will be great distress, unequalled from the beginning of the world until now – and never to be equalled again. If those days had not been cut short, no one would survive, but for the sake of the elect those days will be shortened.
>
> (Matthew 24:21-22)

GREAT TRIBULATION

Jesus was describing the great tribulation:

> Immediately after the distress of those days **"the sun will be darkened,** and the moon will not give its light; the stars will fall from the sky, and the heavenly bodies will be shaken."
>
> (Matthew 24:29)

According to Pat we won't be allowed to blow up the planet, and he sees that the only thing that could blot out the sun is the debris caused by an asteroid hitting earth and dust cloud thrown into the atmosphere.[2]

ENDNOTES:

1. https://www.politico.com/news/2020/11/09/republicans-free-fair-elections-435488; By CATHERINE KIM. 09/11/2020 05:00 PM EST. Accessed 12.12.20

2. https://www.youtube.com/watch?v=dF5izJ9KCug

❖

CHAPTER 5

Open Letter of Conviction

THE SPIRITUAL CLIMATE FACING THIS WORLD

This is the 1st of two open letters, from Italian Archbishop Carlo Maria Viganò. His letters to the former president of the US, reveal insight into the spiritual climate facing the world, not just America.

As follows,

OPEN LETTER
TO THE PRESIDENT OF THE UNITED STATES OF
AMERICA
DONALD J. TRUMP

June 7, 2020
Holy Trinity Sunday

Mr. President,

"In recent months we have been witnessing the formation of two opposing sides that I would call Biblical: the children of light and the children of darkness. The children of light constitute the most conspicuous part of humanity, while the children of darkness represent an absolute minority.

And yet the former are the object of a sort of discrimination, which places them in a situation of moral inferiority with respect to their adversaries, who often hold strategic positions in government, in politics, in the economy and in the media. In an apparently inexplicable way, the good are held hostage by the wicked and by those who help them either out of self-interest or fearfulness.

These two sides, which have a Biblical nature, follow the clear separation between the **offspring of the Woman and the offspring of the Serpent.** On the one hand, there are those who, although they have a thousand defects and weaknesses, are motivated by the desire to do good, to be honest, to raise a family, to engage in work, to give prosperity to their homeland, to help the needy, and, in obedience to the Law of God, to merit the Kingdom of Heaven.

On the other hand, there are those who serve themselves, who do not hold any moral principles, who want to demolish the family and the nation, exploit workers to make themselves unduly wealthy, foment internal divisions and wars, and accumulate power and money: for them the fallacious illusion of temporal well-being will one day – if they do not repent – yield to the terrible fate that awaits them, far from God, in eternal damnation.

In society, Mr. President, these two opposing realities co-exist as eternal enemies, just as God and Satan are eternal enemies. And it appears that the children of darkness – whom we may easily identify with the deep state which you wisely oppose and which is fiercely waging war against you in these days – have decided to show their cards, so to speak, by now revealing their plans. They seem to be so certain of already having everything under control that they have laid aside that circumspection that until now had at least partially concealed their true intentions.

The investigations already under way will reveal the true responsibility of those who managed the COVID emergency not only in the area of health care but also in politics, the economy, and the media. **We will probably find that in this colossal operation of social engineering there are people who have decided the fate of humanity,** arrogating to themselves the right to act against the will of citizens and their representatives in the governments of nations.

We will also discover that the riots in these days were provoked by those who, seeing that the virus is inevitably fading and that the social alarm of the pandemic is waning, necessarily have had to provoke civil disturbances, because they would be followed by repression, which, although legitimate, could be condemned as an unjustified aggression against the population.

The same thing is also happening in Europe, in perfect synchrony. It is quite clear that the use of street protests is instrumental to the purposes of those who would like to see someone elected in the upcoming presidential elections who embodies the goals of the deep state and who expresses those goals faithfully and with conviction.

It will not be surprising if, in a few months, we learn once again that hidden behind these acts of vandalism and violence there are **those who hope to profit from the dissolution of the social order so as to build a world without freedom: Solve et Coagula, as the Masonic adage teaches.**

Although it may seem disconcerting, the opposing alignments I have described are also found in religious circles. **There are faithful Shepherds who care for the flock of Christ, but there are also mercenary infidels who seek to scatter the flock** and hand the sheep over to be devoured by ravenous wolves. It is not surprising that these mercenaries are allies of the children of darkness and hate the children of light: **just as there is a deep state, there is also a deep church that betrays its duties and forswears its proper commitments before God. Thus the Invisible Enemy, whom good rulers fight against in public affairs, is also fought against by good shepherds in the ecclesiastical sphere.**

It is a **spiritual battle,** which I spoke about in my recent Appeal, which was published on May 8.

For the first time, the United States has in you a President who courageously defends the right to life, who is not ashamed to denounce the persecution of Christians throughout the world, who speaks of Jesus Christ and the right of citizens to freedom of worship. Your participation in the March for Life, and more recently your proclamation of the month of April as National Child Abuse Prevention Month, are **actions that confirm which side you wish to fight on. And I dare to believe that both of us are on the same side in this battle, albeit with different weapons.**

For this reason, I believe that the attack to which you were subjected after your visit to the National Shrine of Saint John Paul II is part of the orchestrated media narrative which seeks not to fight racism and bring social order, but to aggravate dispositions; **not to bring justice, but to legitimize violence and crime; not to serve the truth, but to favour one political faction.**

And it is disconcerting that there are Bishops – such as those whom I recently denounced – who, by their words, prove that they are aligned on the opposing side. **They are subservient to the deep state, to globalism, to aligned thought, to the New World Order which they invoke ever more frequently in the name of a universal brotherhood which has nothing Christian about it, but which evokes the Masonic ideals of those who want to dominate the world by driving God out of the courts, out of schools, out of families, and perhaps even out of churches.**

The American people are mature and have now understood how much **the mainstream media does not want to spread the truth but seeks to silence and distort it,** spreading the lie that is useful for the purposes of their masters. However, it is important that the good – who are the majority – wake up from their sluggishness and do not accept being deceived by a minority of dishonest people with unavowable purposes.

It is necessary that the good, the children of light, come together and make their voices heard. What more effective way is there to do this, Mr. President, than by prayer, asking the Lord to protect you, the United States, and all of humanity from this enormous attack of the Enemy?

Before the power of prayer, the deceptions of the children of darkness will collapse, their plots will be revealed, their betrayal will be shown, their frightening power will end in nothing, brought to light and exposed for what it is: an infernal deception.

Mr. President, my prayer is constantly turned to the beloved American nation, where I had the privilege and honour of being sent by Pope Benedict XVI as Apostolic Nuncio. In this dramatic and decisive hour for all of humanity, I am praying for you and also for all those who are at your side in the government of the United States. I trust that the American people are united with me and you in prayer to Almighty God.

United against the Invisible Enemy of all humanity, I bless you and the First Lady, the beloved American nation, and all men and women of good will."[1]

NOTE: *I placed the 2nd Open Letter by The **Archbishop Carlo Maria Viganò**, dated October 25, 2020, in my first book, "The Great Reset Deception."*

President Trump's Official Twitter Response:

So honoured by Archbishop Viganò's incredible letter to me. I hope everyone, religious or not, reads it!
　　　　　　　　　　　—@realDonaldTrump [Twitter.com][2]

There is always push back of course,

> The views put forth by Archbishop Viganò in his letter to the president are **far outside the mainstream of U.S. and global Catholicism.**
> — The Jesuit Review

Brief background on Archbishop Viganò:

According to Michael J. O'Loughlin and contributor Colleen Dulle, of The Jesuit Review, *"Archbishop Carlo Maria Viganò, a former Vatican ambassador to the United States... in a series of missives in recent years... blamed the church's sexual abuse crisis on gay priests, accused Pope Francis of championing schism and called for the pope to resign because of his alleged mishandling of abuse allegations..."*

Cardinal Joseph Tobin, who leads the Archdiocese of Newark, reacted by saying that the Archbishop's letter against the Pope was filled with *"factual errors, innuendo and fearful ideology."*

Weighing in on current events through *"letters and interviews with sympathetic journalists,"* according to O'Loughlin the Archbishop made claims that Masons and Jesuits were *"infiltrating"* the church and that Pope Francis was *"divisive and destructive."*

He goes on to write, *"Archbishop Viganò accused unnamed bishops of being 'subservient' to the deep state and advocating 'globalism' a term that some say carries anti-Semitic history."* Prior to the open letter for Trump in June 2020, there was another manifesto that was signed by several Catholics and led by Archbishop Viganò, which claimed that the coronavirus pandemic was part of one big attempt to create *"a world government beyond all control."*

NO LIGHTWEIGHT

While mocking Viganò's assertions of "Masonic plots" and "deep state conspiracies," these writers ultimately admitted the Archbishop held significant clout: *"The views put forth by Archbishop Viganò in his letter to the president are far outside the mainstream of U.S. and global Catholicism. But because of his past service in the Vatican's diplomatic corps, Archbishop Viganò's words carry some institutional heft."*

Citing various scandals that Viganò was supposedly the architect of, they claim that "he served as the papal ambassador to the United States... between 2011 to 2016," and that his appointment to the United States was *"a form of exile after he spoke out against corruption he saw present in Pope Benedict XVI's inner circle, concerns made public in the so-called Vatileaks scandal."*

In addition to this, Vatican reporter Christopher Lamb, in an attempt to discredit Viganò, went as far as to say that during his time in Washington, Archbishop Viganò *"aligned himself with culture warriors and anti-Francis supporters."*

Apparently Viganò blamed the sexual abuse crisis on *"gay priests"* and accused Pope Francis of *"defending homosexual clergy who committed serious sexual abuses against minors or adults..."* And that *"homosexuality was the root cause of the church's sexual abuse problem."* Other observers levelled the accusation that Viganò, *"took advantage of the sexual abuse crisis to settle old scores and that his concern for victims was secondary."*

According to The Washington Post, during an interview with him in 2019, Viganò supposedly doubled down on his claims against Pope Francis saying that a "gay mafia" comprised of bishops was ***"sabotaging all efforts at reform."***

The article ends sympathetically of Pope Francis, "While Archbishop Viganò continues to assail Pope Francis, polls show that U.S. Catholics overall hold him in high esteem, leaving the impact of the Italian archbishop's presidential endorsement an open question."[3]

As to be expected, the mainstream media *(MSM of church politics)*, always act like false prophets, throwing slander and false accusations at any bastion of truth *(see also Nehemiah 6:5-9)*.

ENDNOTES:

1. www.lifesitenews.com; Sat Jun 6, 2020 - 10:26 am EST. Accessed site 14.12.20. https://www.lifesitenews.com/opinion/archbishop-viganos-powerful-letter-to-president-trump-eternal-struggle-between-good-and-evil-playing-out-right-now

2. Tweet by 45th President of the United States of America; @realDonaldTrump - 11th June 2020. 44.4K retweets - 88.6 million followers. https://twitter.com/realDonaldTrump/status/1270842639903006720

3. Some excerpts taken in part from an article in "America: The Jesuit Review." "Leading Catholic journal of opinion in the US - for discerning Catholics - since 1909"! Michael J. O'Loughlin is the national correspondent for America / Accessed 14.12.20. (Colleen Dulle contributed to this report). Copyright © 2020 America Press Inc. All Rights Reserved. https://www.americamagazine.org/faith/2020/06/11/president-trump-tweeted-about-archbishop-vigano-so-who-he

❖

CHAPTER 6

Defining Democratic Socialism

MODERN LANGUAGE IS DECEPTIVE

I watched Alexandria Ocasio-Cortez on YouTube the other day, wearing her, "Tax the Rich" T-shirt.

I understand why some people - especially younger generations - are switched on to her passion and charisma. She is wide-eyed and fresh off the block, ready for action. She's not jaded and tired yet, like so many, and she actually believes her own rhetoric. That I guess is the most attractive thing about it. She actually believes what she is saying.

She is convincing because she herself is convinced by it - either her acting skills are off the charts or her puppet masters have her so well trained like a poodle, jumping through their hoops, or this girl is so on fire that they just let her loose. Like an arrow in their bow, they just let her rip.

But its dangerous what she is touting. Someone can be utterly deluded while thinking everyone else is deluded. You can be sincere but sincerely wrong. So her enthusiastic, fresh faced appeal can be quite seductive, but she is using and being used.

It's like the matrix, a complete alter universe. Both sides of the same coin see things so vastly different to one another. It's tribal diatribe and hyperbole that's being stoked, like fire. Where will it lead, again perhaps civil war?

THE PRISON OF TWO IDEAS

In the UK there are marches in defiance of lockdowns and mask wearing. Those in the march say many more people are dying of poverty and untreated health issues for fear of catching Covid-19 - while those on the other side of the street wearing masks scream out - "No - you are killing people, because you won't wear masks. You're selfish." Two opposing views creates the prison of two ideas.

We are in a dangerous place. A house divided against it-self cannot stand. We are being set up for a fall. All this is designed to fail.

Jesus knew their thoughts and said to them: "__Any__ kingdom divided against itself will be ruined, and a house divided against itself will fall."

(Luke 11:17)

LANGUAGE DEFINES SOCIALISM

We will explore socialism and the communist takeover in chapter 12 of this book, but the current language that's being used to define socialism is deceptive. Such as the term being used as *Democratic Socialism* - One is from the bottom up and the other is from the top down - it can't be both. You can't have it both ways. But that's what tyranny wants.[1]

Totalitarianism wants it all. Not for you to have it all though. Only the puppet masters, not us. No sir! If you give us money, we have a voice. If you take it from us, we have none. Again, who is listening to the cry of the Venezuelan people?

> *Now there lived in that city a man poor but wise, and he saved the city by his wisdom. But nobody remembered that poor man. So I said, "Wisdom is better than strength." But the poor man's wisdom is despised, and his words are no longer heeded.*
>
> (Ecclesiastes 9:15-16)

> *The poor are shunned by all their relatives---how much more do their friends avoid them! Though the poor pursue them with pleading, they are nowhere to be found.*
>
> (Proverbs 19:7)

Less than ten years ago, you couldn't refer to "socialism" in a positive way and hope to have a career in politics. Socialism was referred to as "the s-word." Now it is affirmed, either explicitly or implicitly, by just about everyone on the left. And amazingly, given socialism's record of failures, the socialists seem to be gaining ground. Why? What makes socialism so attractive to so many? Socialism, according to its proponents, is more democratic and therefore more moral than capitalism.

Leftist filmmaker Michael Moore explains it for us: "Democratic socialism means everyone has a seat at the table and everybody gets a slice of the pie." The famed socialist writer, **Irving Howe,** wrote something similar in his 1982 autobiography: "We believe that the democracy... in our political life should also be extended deeply into economic life."

The basic idea here is that socialism is vindicated through its roots in popular consent. If a majority of people, working through their elected representatives, declares something to be a public entitlement — say, free college or free healthcare — then they are justified in extracting resources from those who create wealth to pay for it.

As **Nathan Robinson argues** in his book, *Why You Should Be a Socialist,* the moral imperative is to place the economy under the control of "the people." Sounds good — at least, superficially — until you dig a bit below the surface.

DIRECT CONTROL

First, what direct control do "the people" really have over any government institution? What control do the British people have over the National Health Service? What control do Americans have over the Department of Motor Vehicles or the U.S. Post Office? The answer, of course, is none. Given its practical impossibility, genuine popular control over government institutions is a mirage.

Second, what if 51% of Americans vote to confiscate the resources of a single person — say, Bill Gates? Does that make it right? Under an authoritarian socialist government, a single dictator seizes the fruits of your labor. Everyone is against that. Under democratic socialism, a majority does. The end result is the same: you've been robbed.

The fundamental problem with democratic socialism, however, is its assumption that in a free market system, the economy is not under the control of the people. This is exactly the opposite of how things work. Let me explain.

Each of us, are not only citizens; we are also consumers. These are overlapping categories: every citizen is a consumer, and every consumer is also a citizen. The consumer, like the citizen, is a voter. As citizens, we vote once every two or four years. As consumers, we vote many times a day.

The citizen votes with a ballot, which costs him nothing, accept the inconvenience of going to the polls. The consumer votes with his money, which costs him a lot — all the time and effort he put in to earn that money. Only a fraction of citizens are eligible to vote at the ballot box, but every consumer votes in the marketplace — even felons, even children. Illegal aliens cannot vote for political candidates, but they, too, vote with their money.

Moreover, citizens participate in a system of representative democracy — their views are filtered through the politicians who represent them. Consumers, by contrast, vote in a system of direct democracy. If you prefer an Audi to a Lexus or the Apple iPhone to the Samsung Galaxy, you don't have to elect some other guy to exercise these preferences; you do it directly yourself — by paying for them.

Here we see the secret of how those billionaires like Jeff Bezos got so rich. We made them rich! The inequality that socialists complain about is the result of popular mandate. Want fewer billionaires? Stop buying their stuff!

POPULAR PARTICIPATION

Free markets work not through "greed" or "exploitation," but by satisfying our wants — and the most successful entrepreneurs are those who anticipate our wants even before we have them. No one wrote Steve Jobs, asking him to make a phone that took pictures, allowed people to text messages and listen to music. He conceived it and built it before we knew we couldn't live without it.

Market economies involve a level of popular participation and democratic consent that politics can only envy. We don't need to extend democracy from the political to the economic sphere; we already have it. And the moral grounding of free markets, just like that of our political system, is in the will of the people — in the latter case, a will expressed only on Election Day; in the former case, a will expressed deliberately, emphatically, constantly.

We don't need socialism because we already have something more moral and more democratic. It's called capitalism.

By Dinesh D'Souza[2]

DARKNESS CANNOT
COMPREHEND THE LIGHT

I saw on twitter the other day that someone had posted a picture of a van traveling ahead of them on the highway, with a large anti-Trump slogan too crude to repeat. The person, who posted it on Twitter, put this counter statement underneath that read:

Darkness cannot comprehend the light "The light shineth in darkness; and the darkness comprehended it not" (John 1:5 KJV).

How true. This reminds me of the tangible darkness in Egypt *"…that could be felt."* This is what happens when 100% of the light is extracted. Consider what life would be like. Exodus verse 23 says that *"No one could see anyone else or move about for three days…"*

It's darkness that shuts people down and restricts their movements, not the light. If one political system brings prosperity and freedom, but the other brings about poverty, abortion and lockdowns - it's easy to perceive what side they're on.

Then the LORD said to Moses, "Stretch out your hand toward the sky so that darkness spreads over Egypt — darkness that can be felt." So Moses stretched out his hand toward the sky, and total darkness covered all Egypt for three days. No one could see anyone else or move about for three days. Yet all the Israelites had light in the places where they lived.

(Exodus 10:21-23)

I saw an artist's depiction of this once. In the distance you could see where the Israelis lived, it looked warm, welcoming and all lit up. But where the Egyptians lived, the darkness was completely engulfing. Even their lit candles inside their homes struggled to give off any light at all... It was a powerful image. **Darkness that can be felt is very oppressive indeed.**

A GOVERNMENT SPIRIT

If the Antichrist is ultimately a government spirit that takes over world governments to shut down Christians in the same way that Hitler took over government and Nero took over government, then **the false prophet isn't some guy who's on Christian television prophesying falsely; the false prophet is the voice that supports the emergence of the Antichrist, and that's media.**

ENDNOTES:

1. https://dennisprager.com/new-prageru-video-capitalism-or-socialism-which-is-more-democratic/; https://www.prageru.com/video/capitalism-or-socialism-which-one-is-more-democratic/

2. https://assets.ctfassets.net/qnesrjodfi80/5YIYzU4vEYkHVREFQf sCsK/2cbda4425def154dd99d414604cabd7b/DSouza-Capitalism_ or_Socialism-Which_One_Is_More_Democratic-Transcript.pdf; https://www.prageru.com/video/democratic-socialism-is-still-socialism/

3. Scripture quotations marked KJV are taken from the King James Version of the Bible.

❖

CHAPTER 7

The Definition of Media

NUMBER ONE SPIRITUAL GATEWAY

In my book "Media Spiritual Gateway," written by my wife and I, we can see in chapter one, the Hebrew definition of *Hittite* was all about FEAR. Mentioned first out of seven, for good reason, as no other spiritual gateway holds as much power as the media.[1]

Let's face it; we live in the era of fake news! It's always existed, but never been quite so prominent. Today it's an all-out-war between fact and political fiction. The media has been sabotaged by political activism. Gone are the days of impartiality and objective unbiased reporting, with many sources saying that true journalism is dead.

Sensationalism keeps the cable news channels on air; embellishing the facts ensures entertainment value and viewership 24/7 *(first coined as Yellow Journalism)*. Citizen journalism now means that EVERYONE HAS A CAMERA and Robojournalism is the new necessity, to keep up with demand.

FEAR HAS POWER

Fear has great sway to influence everything that goes on in society; locally, nationally and internationally, including stock markets and the global economy.

However according to Revelations 21:7-8, we are destined to conquer and not be defeated or beaten down by fear. In fact if we surrender our lives to the propaganda of fear, then God is not pleased at all.

So how do we define the media? The dictionary says that it's: "the main means of mass communication *(broadcasting, publishing, and the Internet)* regarded collectively." The platforms it uses are radio and TV stations, news networks and outlets, newspapers and magazines, Internet websites, opinion sites, blogs and much more.

News travels faster than the speed of light in today's world. It can circle the globe countless times before we can count on one hand! The Internet makes news not only travel faster but also greatly more accessible and widens the audience to even younger demographics, unparalleled to any other time in history.

CENSORSHIP, MONOPOLY AND GROUPTHINK

Part of the media's power is its ability to censor information in order to control the narrative. Companies such as Facebook and Google for example, hold dangerous monopolies; even have as much revenue as some countries do! In fact Investopedia is quoted as saying, "Google's revenue beats the GDP of several major countries." Calling the company, "Google Nation" and its employees, "corporate citizens."[2]

Media can incite public outrage over political issues while at the same time muffle stories that warrant massive exposure. Interviews can be deliberately *spliced* to misrepresent and mislead.

Fake outrage can be incited. Like the crowd that demanded the release of Barabbas opposed to Jesus, *(perhaps the very same crowd who shouted* "Hosanna," *not so long before!)* Media counts on the feckless and spineless principles of any *crowd.* Today, this can be referred to as *groupthink,* which according to the dictionary is, ***"the practice of thinking or making decisions as a group, resulting typically in unchallenged, poor-quality decision-making."***[3]

Misinformation can be deliberately fed to the public so that by the time it's been officially *retracted* or *corrected,* the damage has long been done. Stories can be spiked or widely disseminated, depending on who is pulling the strings at the top. Partisan agendas, special interests, lobbying, bribery, elite conspiracy, cover-up and corruption, are all part of media's territory.

So it's safe to say that media, as a news outlet, is not a reliable source of impartial facts any longer, but a mechanism for *indoctrination.* Media has always flirted with danger because of its ability to shape public opinion. However, in today's environment and aggressive censorship practices, freedom of speech is either - public enemy No.1 or an elaborate myth.

Needless to say that media's reporting is not always accurate and though the use of *propaganda* is not new, it still has a new handle - **Fake-News!** Nothing exposes fake-news like politics, where elections are won and lost, based on the information that is fed to the public. The same public who take their generously cultivated *opinions* to the ballot box! Propaganda has been rebranded for today's savvier audience.

LEFT LEANING MEDIA
PUSHES SOCIALISM ON MILLENNIALS + GEN-Z

Conservative news and information services have been elevated in recent times, but they come under heavy fire from the left. Now more than ever, in this politically charged climate, *misrepresentation* is endemic. Take for instance socialism, which is trending specifically amongst Millennials and GEN-Z, because they have no way of grasping the consequences of going down that particular path. They have no go-to experience in their own lifetime, to get up close to.

Learning-by-experience is lost on them because they are experiencing much of this stuff for the first time around and aren't willing to listen to the menacing warnings of history. Naïvely supposing that their new and enlightened version of socialism can offer modern improvements on a failed system that has arguably never worked, anywhere in the world that it has been implemented, to date *(just ask any struggling Venezuelan who can't afford toilet paper, if they agree!)*

In fact, we are going to see more of a push towards socialism as time progresses, especially from the far-left. And the more "left" of the political spectrum that the media leans, the more favourable they are going to become. After all, socialism is a control mechanism. It makes it easier to control people. While history teaches not everyone acquiesces, especially when they *realise* they're being exploited. The mainstream media that used to stand up against such things are more and more in the bag.

The tall and short of it is this: media is a major information gateway and in the wrong hands can create a dangerous monopoly. We have to offer an alternative.

We have a choice to make. Either we point out everything that's wrong with media or we turn the tables and control this unopposed force, for good. To build up media empires that use these vastly influential means to herald the truth of God.

ENDNOTES:

1. "Media, Spiritual Gateway" by Drs Alan and Jennifer Pateman, Copyright © 2018, Published by APMI Publications

2. https://www.investopedia.com/articles/investing/061115/googles-revenue-beats-gdp-several-major-countries.asp?ad=dirN&qo=investopediaSiteSearch&qsrc=0&o=40186

3. https://en.oxforddictionaries.com/definition/groupthink

❖

CHAPTER 8

Joseph – God's Catalyst

NOT SWAYED BY THE CULTURE

First let's consider what aided Joseph to live in the times that he did and not be swayed by the culture. He was a man of God who became second only to Pharaoh. His position was a result of divine strategy, even though he lived in a deeply pagan society *(polytheistic and ritualistic not Judaeo-Christian)*. In other words his boss and counterparts didn't share his belief system!

> *So Pharaoh said to Joseph, "I hereby put you in charge of the whole land of Egypt." Then Pharaoh took his signet ring from his finger and put it on Joseph's finger. He dressed him in robes of fine linen and put a gold chain around his neck. He had him ride in a chariot as his second-in-*

command, and people shouted before him, "Make way!" Thus he put him in charge of the whole land of Egypt.

Then Pharaoh said to Joseph, "I am Pharaoh, but without your word no one will lift hand or foot in all Egypt." Pharaoh gave Joseph the name Zaphenath-Paneah and gave him Asenath daughter of Potiphera, priest of On, to be his wife. And Joseph went throughout the land of Egypt.

(Genesis 41:41-45)

What's your point? Joseph had to function deep inside an ancient Egyptian system, without it getting deep inside of him. He remained righteous and divinely positioned in order to help serve and save that society *(Not to mention, preserve the lineage of Jesus Christ).*

So, Joseph was God's change-agent at a crucial juncture in history. He was the lynchpin and catalyst for systemic change, without being changed himself.

THIS IS OUR MODEL

We are to go into the market place, where corruption dwells and allow God to raise us up. We need to understand God's positioning and bring His righteous influence from deep within and from the top down.

Some of us are like modern Trojan horses, uniquely anointed and positioned to infiltrate the world's system from the inside out *(Not just window-shopping from the outside-looking-in).* **We've got to get *inside* the culture in order to impact it - not vice-versa:**

Bear in mind though, that Joseph's preparation for this position was intense. Why? He had to be able to handle it. His foundations had to run deep, so not to be toppled by the very culture he was injected into. Our God is a master strategist. He gets results, if we follow and obey His plan and not our own egos.

Pharaoh may not have changed much. Egyptian society might not have changed much, but God got His desired result. So not everyone out there in society is going to be saved, just because we show up, still God's strategy and plan will play out, all the same.

Today God has no less ability to position his change-agents, who can go "viral" into the blood stream of society, the culture and media.

GOD'S PLAN AND PURPOSE!

In Deuteronomy the **Hittites** were the first of a list of seven very strong nations that needed be conquered in the Promised Land. And what propagates fear, terror and dismay more than the media? *(For example entertainment is fiction but News is based on facts).*

> *Seven nations, all greater and mightier than you are: the Hittites, the Girgashites, the Amorites, the Canaanites, the Perizzites, the Hivites, the Jebusites. When the Lord your God delivers them over to you to be destroyed, do a complete job of it.*
>
> *(Deuteronomy 7:1-2 TLB)*

In the last segment, we considered Joseph and the position he was given in Egyptian society next to Pharaoh because of the gift that God had given him of interpreting dreams. Beyond dreams Joseph had much more to offer and bring to the table. He was a great leader who knew how to manage things well.

He was an organiser, fixer and problem solver. He handled responsibility well and got results, which benefited everyone. So interpreting dreams was just the tip of the iceberg.

The idea of going into the secular arena to bring change is synonymous with the example Joseph set. God so loved the world that He gave. We could say that He gave Joseph to Pharaoh and to the Egyptian people, in order to help avert a major humanitarian catastrophe. There was much more to it of course, but for our purposes here, we know that Joseph was positioned, not just for personal gain or legacy; he was fulfilling the very purposes of God in his generation, which made way for the next:

> *We know that all things work together for good to them that love God, to them who are the* **called according to his purpose.**
>
> *(Romans 8:28 KJVS)*

> *We are confident that God is able to orchestrate everything to work toward something good and beautiful when we love Him and* **accept His invitation to live according to His plan.**
>
> *(Romans 8:28 VOICE)*

God has a plan. But a plan always requires strategy. We are not groping in the dark or beating the air. There is a significant plan and when we come to God, we are yielding our lives to that purpose. It's a life of personal sacrifice. It's only as we lay it all down, that God can use us.

> *Offer your bodies as a **living sacrifice,** holy and pleasing to God, this is your true and proper worship.*
>
> *(Romans 12:1)*

Above all, my concern is that people live according to God's plan and not their own. This is authentic service. Everything outside of that is nothing more than self-service and false-humility.

TRUE HUMILITY COUNTERS NARCISSISM

Joseph was elevated from a pit of consecration:

It takes great humility to stay dedicated in elevated positions. Think of Daniel. He too knew how to function in a secular environment but stay inwardly holy. He was not a man of compromise, what you compromise to keep, you'll always lose anyway!

> *Humble yourselves, therefore, under God's mighty hand, that he may lift you up in due time.*
>
> *(1 Peter 5:6-7)*

> *He gives His grace [His undeserved favour] to the* **humble [those who give up self-importance].**
>
> *(Proverbs 3:34 AMP)*

It's common knowledge that "God goes against the wilful proud; **God gives grace to the willing humble."**

(James 4:6 MSG)

All of you, clothe yourselves with humility toward one another, because, "God opposes the proud but **shows favour to the humble."**

(1 Peter 5:5)

So how do we influence the media? The answer: there must be an army of Josephs and Daniels to flood the market! Men and women of personal sacrifice, who'll sacrifice personal gain for a higher purpose, in the face of cultural narcissism.

CULTURAL PENETRATION

He said unto them, **Go ye into all the world,** *and preach the gospel (Kingdom Truths and Principles) to every creature.*

(Mark 16:15 KJV)

Men shall be lovers of their own selves... lovers of pleasures more than lovers of God; having a form of godliness, but denying the power thereof: **from such turn away.**

(2 Timothy 3:4 KJV)

Herein is our dilemma. How do we simultaneously, **"go INTO all the world"** and **"...turn away"** at the same time? How do we breach the culture without being snared by it? It presents us with a legitimate paradox. The only answer can be that we must *penetrate* the heart of the culture without it penetrating ours. Making no treaties and remaining solely surrendered to God.

In Mark 16:15 the original language for, *"go **into** all the world,"* directly refers to *"penetration."* The Israelites may have left Egypt but Egypt had certainly not left them. So their hearts readily gravitated back to what influenced them the most, *(and who knew cucumbers and onions tasted so good?)*

We remember the fish we ate in Egypt at no cost – also the cucumbers, melons, leeks, onions and garlic. But now we have lost our appetite; we never see anything but this manna!

(Numbers 11:5-6)

Thinking of the country they had left, they would have had opportunity to return.

(Hebrews 11:14-16)

In short, nothing can bring lasting change without penetration:

The entrance *of thy words giveth light; it giveth understanding…*

(Psalm 119:130 KJV)

We must penetrate the culture, using media, **allowing God to affect the culture forever with His incorruptible seed,** it never returns to Him void.

ENDNOTES:

1. Scripture quotations marked AMP are taken from the Amplified® Bible, Copyright © 2015 by The Lockman Foundation. Used by permission. (www.Lockman.org)

2. Scripture quotations marked KJV are taken from the King James Version of the Bible.

3. Scripture quotations marked KJVS are taken from the Strong's Concordance with KJV. Taken from the TecartaBible App, © 2017 Tecarta, Inc. Version 7.11.5. Used by permission. All rights reserved.

4. Scripture quotations marked MSG are taken from The Message. Copyright © 1993, 1994, 1995, 1996, 2000, 2001, 2002. Used by permission of NavPress Publishing Group.

5. Scripture quotations marked TLB are taken from The Living Bible. Copyright © 1971 by Tyndale House Foundation. Used by permission of Tyndale House Publishers Inc., Carol Stream, Illinois 60188. All rights reserved.

6. Scripture quotations marked VOICE are taken from The Voice™. Copyright © 2008 by Ecclesia Bible Society. Used by permission. All rights reserved.

❖

CHAPTER 9

Two Separate Spheres

BOTH LEGS HAVE EQUAL FOOTING

It was the risen One who handed down to us such gifted leaders—some emissaries, some prophets, some evangelists, as well as some pastor-teachers—so that God's people would be thoroughly equipped to minister and build up the body of the Anointed One. These ministries will continue until we are unified in faith and filled with the knowledge of the Son of God, until we stand mature in His teachings and fully formed in the likeness of the Anointed, our Liberating King *(Ephesians 4:11-13 VOICE)*.

I liked some teaching that I heard from Dutch Sheets some years ago that brilliantly contrasted the two separate spheres of operation that the Church has been called to. I'll unpack and explain.

Not unlike our own bodies, Christ's body has two large legs to stand upon: "Oikos" and "Ecclesia." These two Greek words represent the relational and family aspects of the Church versus the authoritative and legislative (*governing*) aspects of the Church. Both legs have equal footing and create balance for the entire body.

> People often tell me, "Quit talking about all the warfare stuff." Because they just want to focus on the power of loving each other. All the pastoral people say, "If you'd just love each other everything would be okay." Well, we loved each other through the Charismatic Movement and we lost America, because we didn't understand that we're an "ecclesia" called to disciple a nation.
>
> — Dutch Sheets

This is a powerful point. Children never have to be taught how to be naughty, but good. Even Jesus, Who was without sin, still had to learn obedience. That's how we know He was human (*Hebrews 5:8; 1 Timothy 2:5*).

Consider how we love our children, yet still discipline them. God said, "I discipline those I love." Yes, it sounds like a mixed message when you're little, *"pain means I love you!"*

The truth is, you wouldn't waste your time trying to discipline little Johnny next door or noisy Suzy down the street, because they're not your responsibility; if however they're living under your roof and your responsibility, then sure.

My son, do not make light of the Lord's discipline, and do not lose heart when he rebukes you, because **the Lord disciplines the one he loves, and he chastens everyone he <u>accepts as his son</u>**.

(Hebrews 12:5-6)

DELINQUENT PARENTING

So basically, if someone has the jurisdiction to discipline you *(not oppress you)*, according to Hebrews 12:5-6 this represents a recognition of responsibility, love and acceptance. Conversely *delinquent* parenting is *absent* parenting. In other words, the parents that take zero responsibility prove they *couldn't care less*. Thus the Internet's been raising an entire generation of kids left at home alone, looking for company, stimuli and entertainment online *(babysitting 1.0.1 – except for the lack of discipline involved)*.

Take my own children for example, during their formative years I had to nurture and love them simultaneously while having to teach, steer and discipline them. The ultimate tight-rope, a little too far one way or the other and you've got problems, but no one said parenting would be easy.

Lots of *"nurture"* without *"discipline"* creates privileged-snowflakes, on the other hand the *well-adjusted-types* don't just happen by accident. Usually they've been raised well. Or, as we'd say in the UK, *"they've been brought up rather than dragged up,"* which can mean their parents did a decent job of rearing them.

With this in mind, now consider Jesus. He's the perfect balance between The Great Shepherd and Commander in

Chief. We must know how to deal with either. As Dutch Sheets said, *"You better know when you're dealing with the Commander in Chief and when you're dealing with the Great Shepherd. The Great Shepherd will pat you on the back but the Commander in Chief will kick you in the backside."* How true. I think I've had my fair share of those, but hallelujah that makes me a SON.

Now when it comes to the Body of Christ in general, we must contrast the two spheres:

- **Family** *(love through relationship)* "Oikos"
- **Government** *(love through authority)* "Ecclesia"

So what does it look like when both spheres work together?

We could picture it like this; the relational, loving, family side must work in equality with the equipping, active, governing side of the Church. One is content maintaining the status quo; the other is only content when it sees growth and development. One values relational harmony while the other breakthrough and achievement.

- **In relationship** we represent God's family, body, bride and flock
- **In government** we represent His ambassadors, legislators and military *(warriors and soldiers)*

Dutch Sheets continues,

We've been struggling to enter this side. We haven't done it well. There's going to be a tremendous tension between the two... While we were getting people saved the world around us was discipling America. They took over government, and they took over education and they took over media, the arts and the entertainment and we're going to take it back!

Now consider who Jesus is in relation to us:

- **In relationship** Jesus is our Shepherd, Groom, Elder, Firstborn Brother etc.
- **In government** Jesus is our King, Lord and Master

In the big picture we must consider the five-fold ministry. Such gifts were never meant to compete or compare. They go where they're needed. For example the gifts vital for family are: Evangelist *(to multiply and grow the family)*, Pastor *(to care for the family)* and Teacher *(to teach the family)*. Note: The apostolic and prophetic input is also necessary to the family, but not as much.

On the governing side of the Church, the gifts most vital are: The Apostle, Prophet and Teacher. The Apostle is going to oversee the whole operation, *(to ensure the fulfilment of the commission, that we govern well and that we function well as army)*. The prophet discerns timing and directs. The teachers teach and train.

Back on the family side of the Church, Jesus is the Head Administrator, Coordinator, High Priest and Good Shepherd. While on the governing side He's Chief Apostle, General Overseer and Bishop.

According to Dutch Sheets:

If all we have is a household and a family, somebody else is going to write the laws. If the Church doesn't rise up to that mountain and make itself known through spiritual warfare and filling those positions, we can worship all we want, be a nice little happy family, but somebody else is going to write the laws.

In the 60's, 70s, 80s and 90s we lost our voice. They mock us when we try to have a voice. But I have news for them: Court is in session! God is about to give us back our voice.[1]

ENDNOTES:

1. https://www.youtube.com/watch?v=Lre6wso8tRs; https://tv.gloryofzion.org; This video is published with permission from Chuck Pierce. https://bit.ly/2TRObAR info@kingofkingswc.com

2. Scripture quotations marked VOICE are taken from The Voice™. Copyright © 2008 by Ecclesia Bible Society. Used by permission. All rights reserved.

CHAPTER 10

Will Britons be Micro-chipped?

SUPER SURVEILLANCE

VIRAL IMAGE CLAIMS TO SHOW UK GOVERNMENT LETTER ABOUT PROPOSED MANDATORY MICROCHIPS.

Recently an image went viral on Facebook that showed a letter, supposedly from the U.K. government concerning a "proposed policy" that would require all U.K. residents to be micro chipped from 2021 onwards.

As it turns out, this was deemed "false," it was quickly "debunked" right across the Internet – with speed! After the rush to diffuse it, should we just exhale and say, *"Phew, that was close! Now we can go back to our normal lives again."* Really?

Naivety is cute in children perhaps, but not in adults. Most discerning individuals can, without a conspiracy deficiency or addiction; figure out that it's just a matter of "time," because the technology is available and has been for a long time. Public willingness on the other hand is not available. Either something cataclysmic has to take place, to induce compliance - like a pandemic perhaps - or at some point be made mandatory.

Far-fetched science fiction is not so far-fetched any more. Yet, as it stands microchips have been banished to the "conspiracy corner" - until such point perhaps when the threat of severe civil unrest doesn't exist. Or far Left governments and elite globalists get their way and force their utopian dream on the rest of us.

Looking at numerous sites today the verdict on this was unanimous. There is no record of the U.K. government proposing such a policy. A spokesperson for the Cabinet Office confirmed the letter as fake.

But what will the "fact-checkers" be saying in just 5 years from now?

EXCERPT AS FOLLOWS

The letter, which appears to bear the official U.K. government letterhead and Prime Minister Boris Johnson's signature, informs recipients of a proposed policy that would require all residents to receive a radio frequency identification (RFID) microchip starting in 2021. Such implants would be provided and inserted for free through the National Health Service (NHS), according to the letter.

"In a world where we face issues of terrorism, crime and cyber fraud, the RFID microchips will enable law enforcement agencies to track the movements of criminals and terrorists," the alleged letter continues. "It will also hold a unique personal identification number, that once scanned, will allow law enforcement to identify whether that person is: wanted for a crime, an illegal immigrant or a terrorist sympathiser etc."

Accordingly they say, "No such letter was sent by the Prime Minister, it is entirely fake,' Bobby Mayamey, senior press officer of the Cabinet Office confirmed to the Caller in an email."

However, in the spirit of good journalism, this article in checkyourfact.com offers up this little morsel of honesty, *"BioTeq a British company began offering individuals and companies wearable RFID services in 2018, The Guardian reported. Data privacy and health concerns are among some of the worries associated with this new technology, per EuroNews."*[1]

JUST A MATTER OF TIME

At this point in world affairs *(at the time of writing)*, regardless whether it's true or false, it will happen eventually, because the intent is there. No one is fooled about that; it's just a matter of when. But it will happen in our lifetime, that is a given.

But consider what that would mean in the hands of terrorists and criminals. It's naïve to think they wouldn't take full advantage of such technology. If they can hack a bank, they can hack your life.

Back in 2006 there was an article in The Daily Mail entitled: **"Britons could be micro-chipped like dogs in a decade."** That was more than a decade ago and although we have not seen the roll out of mandatory chip technology yet, that doesn't mean that it has not been happening for some time on a smaller scale.

According to the article:

Human beings may be forced to be "micro-chipped" like pet dogs, a shocking official report into the rise of the Big Brother state has warned. The microchips - which are implanted under the skin - allow the wearer's movements to be tracked and store personal information about them.

They could be used by companies who want to keep tabs on an employee's movements or by Governments who want a foolproof way of identifying their citizens - and storing information about them. The prospect of "chip-citizens" - with its terrifying echoes of George Orwell's "Big Brother" police state in the book 1984 - was raised in an official report for Britain's Information Commissioner Richard Thomas into the spread of surveillance technology.

The report, drawn up by a team of respected academics, claims that Britain is a world-leader in the use of surveillance technology and its citizens the most spied-upon in the free world. It paints a frightening picture of what Britain might be like in ten years time unless steps are taken to regulate the use of CCTV and other spy technologies.

The reports editors Dr David Murakami Wood, managing editor of the journal Surveillance and Society and Dr Kirstie

Ball, an Open University lecturer in Organisation Studies, claim that by 2016 our almost every movement, purchase and communication could be monitored by a complex network of interlinking surveillance technologies.

The most contentious prediction is the spread in the use of Radio Frequency Identification (RFID) technology. The RFID chips, which can be detected and read by radio waves, are already used in new UK passports and are also used in the Oyster card system to access the London Transport network. For the past six years European countries have been using RFID chips to identify pet animals.

ALREADY USED IN AMERICA

However, its use in humans has already been trialed in America, where the chips were implanted in 70 mentally-ill elderly people in order to track their movements. And earlier this year a security company in Ohio chipped two of its employees to allow them to enter a secure area. The glass-encased chips were planted in the recipients' upper right arms and "read" by a device similar to a credit card reader.

In their Report on the Surveillance Society, the authors now warn: "The call for everyone to be implanted is now being seriously debated." The authors also highlight the Government's huge enthusiasm for CCTV, pointing out that during the 1990s the Home Office spent 78 per cent of its crime prevention budget – a total of £500 million – on installing the cameras.

There are now 4.2 million CCTV cameras in Britain and the average Briton is caught on camera an astonishing 300 times every day. This huge enthusiasm comes despite official Home Office statistics showing that CCTV cameras have "little effect on crime levels."

They write: "The surveillance society has come about without us realising", adding: "Some of it is essential for providing the services we need: health, benefits, education. Some of it is more questionable. Some of it may be unjustified, intrusive and oppressive."

Yesterday Information Commissioner Richard Thomas, whose office is investigating the Post Office, HSBC, NatWest and the Royal Bank of Scotland over claims they dumped sensitive customer details in the street, said: "Many of these schemes are public sector driven, and the individual has no choice over whether or not to take part."

"People are being scrutinised by having their lives tracked, and are not even aware of it." He has also voiced his concern about the consequences of companies, or Government agencies, building up too much personal information about someone.

He said: "It can stigmatise people. I have worries about technology being used to identify classes of people who present some kind of risk to society. And I think there are real anxieties about that."

Yesterday a spokesman for civil liberties campaigners Liberty said: "We have got nothing about these surveillance technologies in themselves, but it is their potential uses about which there are legitimate fears. Unless their uses are regulated properly, people really could find themselves living in a surveillance society."

"There is a rather scary underlying feeling that people may worry that these microchips are less about being a human being than becoming a barcoded product."[2]

ENDNOTES:

1. https://checkyourfact.com/2020/06/19/fact-check-uk-government-letter-proposed-mandatory-rfid-microchips/; Accessed 15.12.20. 6:36 PM 06/19/2020. Jonathan Fonti | Fact Check Reporter. https://www.bioteq.co.uk; https://www.theguardian.com/technology/2018/nov/11/alarm-over-talks-to-implant-uk-employees-with-microchips; Julia Kollewe. Sun 11 Nov 2018 18.53 GMT. https://www.euronews.com/2020/05/12/will-microchip-implants-be-the-next-big-thing-in-europe

2. By Dan Newling. Last updated at 00:11 30 October 2006. https://www.dailymail.co.uk/news/article-413345/Britons-microchipped-like-dogs-decade.html; Accessed 15.12.20

❖

CHAPTER 11

Microchip Implants

NEXT BIG THING IN EUROPE?

Back in May 2020 they were asking this question. It keeps coming up. The article written for Euronews by Ric Wasserman starts off by asking: "Will microchip implants be the next big thing in Europe?"

If you're an avid reader like me, you'll know that there's nothing new about all this chatter. Talk about implanting humans with micro-chip technology is old news. The stuff of science fiction is getting hotter and hotter and the technology certainly exists. So what's holding it up? According to one source it is because, "Implantation in **humans** remains uncommon, unpopular."

Oh really! Does that imply that once the majority is cool with it and warmed to the idea, then you'll follow through? I think that would be answered in the affirmative. For the authorities, it's a win win scenario and a certain crime buster *(allegedly)*. So when will people be "open" to this idea? It's just a matter of time and clever psychological manipulation, I guess.

SUPER POWERS

According to the article in Euronews: *"Thousands of Swedes have been pioneering the use of futuristic microchips that are implanted under the skin of the hand,"* then there is an image of just that; someone in surgical gloves inserting a chip via syringe, into some random person's hand, *(between the thumb and the index finger).*

Wasserman continues, The technology is used for everyday tasks like accessing your smartphone, opening the front door or setting an alarm.

Those behind the microchips — the size of a rice grain and implanted via a syringe — are working to access other parts of Europe.

Eric Larsen, who leads Biohax Italia, is waiting for approval in Italy from medical centers and the health ministry. He said he expects to implant a chip into about 2,500 people in the first six to eight months in **Milan and Rome.**

Even without health ministry certification, Biohax Italia has already been able to embed these chips into a few hundred people with the help of a medical center.

It is a step towards the future... It is extremely futuristic although it is already happening. This technology was born to help us, to give us small **superpowers**, Larsen told Euronews.

But COVID-19 could make people more apprehensive about their business, Larsen said, due to public concern about the contact tracing applications introduced by governments during the pandemic.

We are seeing that a lot of people in Italy are not happy [with] adding a GPS or something that can track our movement. That might be a danger for us, he explained.

"We are not tracking movements we don't have a GPS inside but I think that a lot of people are not aware of that."

REMOVING THE NEED FOR A WALLET

Swedish IT solutions planner, Martin Lewin, uses the two microchips in his hand for things like logging into the computer, setting the office alarm and launching his LinkedIn profile.

But using them as an alternative to cash or card payments is expected to be the tipping point for the technology.

It's no different than just removing the need for a wallet, removing the need for a keychain, removing the need for all these disconnected tokens that only create risk because if you lose them you lose your identity, said former body piercer Jowan Österlund, who is behind the start-up Biohax International.

"If you lose your key you won't get into your house. If someone else gets your key they can basically claim your house in some countries."

In Sweden, the microchips can be used as a train ticket. But Lewin hopes that he will soon be able to make payments with them.

That's what I hope will become a basic function, he told Euronews. "I look forward to an ecosystem where the chip is able to provide all types of access. Where your identity can be carried with you in a simple way."

But the technology hasn't taken off as quickly as he expected.

It's taken longer than what I thought and hoped. It was three years ago that I got my chip implanted. It looks like it'll be another year before the chip will work for making payments.

Larsen said that in Italy, Biohax is talking to Vodafone and PayPal to attempt to make that happen. A company in the United Kingdom, BioTeq, is also working to create contactless payments with implanted microchips.

Steven Northam, the director of UK firm BioTeq, said this is the "tipping point to 'mass' adoption" as the company receives daily inquiries about "payment implants".

But it seems the technology hasn't moved as fast as some would have expected. Sweden's train operator SJ said they were ending their microchips trial after a small increase over the last two years bringing the total number of users to 3,000.

A spokesperson for SJ said that although they're keeping the technology available, they will move in "another direction."

PEOPLE ARE APPREHENSIVE

The microchips use near field communications (NFC) and radio-frequency identification (RFID) to communicate with a system. They are radio waves read at close contact.

It's "essentially the same" technology that's in your phone or debit card, explains Dr Rob Van Eijk, the managing director for Europe at the Future of Privacy Forum, when you hold it close to a sensor.

It poses the same known data protection issues including the possibility that someone could pick up the signal. "It's similar to listening in to a directional microphone, you can pick up the RFID signal as well," explained Eijk, who used to work for the Dutch Data Protection Authority.

In theory, it could be used in a way that it makes you stand out in a crowd as a means to single you out as an individual in a group...if you're the only one wearing a biochip and everyone else is not wearing them, he added.

It could also get into more complicated data privacy issues if future versions of these chips track your health or other information, Eijk pointed out. The only information you ever got about implants is Hollywood pop culture and when it's Hollywood pop culture, it's either a giant GPS that Arnold Schwarzenegger pulls out of his nose or KGB polonium or a tracking device. So people are apprehensive, said Österlund.

But many of his customers will get these implants simply to launch their LinkedIn accounts to share their profile more quickly. They're surprised to learn that it's cheaper than they imagined at around €150.

Österlund said they are working with partners so that these microchips contain health information. In the event that someone is brought unconscious to the hospital, a paramedic could scan the chip and get information about allergies or preexisting conditions. For now, they're working on regulating the chips in terms of the grade of material used and the level of data protection.

We're pushing legislation to actually enforce and create a regulatory framework around this because we do work in a legal grey zone right now which is good for development and for disruptive technologies and all but this thing is going into people's bodies and staying there so we need to take that responsibility, said Österlund.

He says it's a technology that already exists in at least 20 countries. BioTeq in the United Kingdom has implanted roughly 250 people with microchips.

The implants are not regulated as medical devices and thus can be implanted by anyone, said Northam at BioTeq, but the company only uses doctors to implant them.

Personally I don't see any downside. I know there are people who are worried that they can be traced, but it's a passive technology, so there's nothing you can't have control over yourself, said Lewin.

"It's necessary to go very close so information can be read off the chip. Some believe that getting the implant will be painful but it's about equal to a bee sting."

The popularity of these chips will boil down to what problem is it solving for us, says Eijk at the Future of Privacy Forum. "Look at how quickly we changed from cash money to contactless payments -- that happened in a number of years," he added.

It's a question of whether or not a phone can become so small as to fit under our skin.

But that's the next level. That's not the type of biochip technology that we're talking about now, said Eijk.[1]

In 1998, Kevin Warwick, a British scientist known as "Captain Cyborg," became the first human to receive a microchip implant, according to The Atlantic.

Then in 2018, it had grown and became widespread in tech-forward Sweden, where an estimated 4,000 citizens use microchips implanted in their hands to store emergency contacts and enable easy access to homes, offices and gyms, according to NPR.

There are also no reported instances of involuntary microchip implantation.

Heightened suspicions in recent months:

This is not the first time misinformation about microchips and RFID has proliferated online in the past few months — from claims that the federal government, Bill Gates, and schools will use a vaccine for COVID-19 as a vehicle for microchips, to fears about the presence of RFID chips in bras and tires.

Although at this point in time, experts say there's little reason to fear surreptitious tracking — at least not from a microchip.

We all voluntarily carry around devices that track us just as well as any sort of chipping, Wang said. "We voluntarily give up our information — much more than you could get from some sort of chip."[2]

ENDNOTES:

1. Video editor Christophe Pitiot. Additional sources Alberto De Filippis. https://www.euronews.com/2020/05/12/will-microchip-implants-be-the-next-big-thing-in-europe; Copyright Euronews/ Ric Wasserman. Accessed 15.12.20. By Lauren Chadwick & Ric Wasserman. Last updated: 12/05/2020

2. https://eu.usatoday.com/story/news/factcheck/2020/08/01/fact-check-americans-will-not-receive-microchips-end-2020/5413714002/; Camille Caldera | USA TODAY. Our fact check work is supported in part by a grant from Facebook. Contributing: Mary Landers, Savannah Morning News

❖

CHAPTER 12

The Takeover

A BID FOR WORLD DOMINANCE

In analysing current would events, providing definitions or and terminologies that are easily confused, there is a challenge, **a bid for world dominance.**

For me, every angle of the political spectrum, whether it's coming out of **"Davos and the Great Reset"** or a specialized agency like the **"World Health Organization"** of the United Nations it's one world order.

China, in accordance with its own ancient philosophy, seeing other powers in the sky as a threat that simply must be removed. Now all this looks very troubling, although there's a lot of "white-noise" going on, but they all seem to be going in the same ultimate direction.

Remembering that today's world is vastly different from the one that Karl Marx and others knew. We deal instead with terminologies like "white-privilege" "black lives matter" and militant left-wing activist groups like "antifa" defined as:

> Antifa are fascist anti-fascists. They fight against "fascists" while being fascist themselves. They will destroy your property if you disagree with them.

> Antifa are the purest form of contradiction, hypocrisy, and accidental irony; they are the modern day equivalent of Nazis. Example: "Hey I'm antifa, I'll pepper spray you for not conforming to my socialist/communist/anarchist ideology."[1]

I don't want to get ahead of myself here, so we're going to look at certain key political terms and define each of them briefly, one by one. There is a danger, that in the event of apologetics, when we try and confront issues, we end up using terminologies that we don't fully understand.

While doing this, we want to keep our focus on China, with its One Party Rule (CCP), the roots to its Communism and its growing influence around the world. Each definition should help shed light on China's ruling party's behaviour and help us better understand its motivations.

CHINA'S TAKEN THE GLOVES OFF

Firstly, but briefly we'll look at the history of Communism. Which is important, to grasp where China is headed. Notice that since the Covid-19 pandemic, China has grown bolder and much more aggressive than before, It would seem, that China has certainly taken its gloves off!

The following definitions will be in this order:

1. Leftism
2. Liberalism
3. Socialism
4. Communism

We'll start with leftism and work our way down the list, in order of severity – to end with democracy. Many folks throw terminologies around like there is no tomorrow. AND although such definitions are currently in a state of flux or being re-defined, we'll seek not to confuse them. For example a liberal is not a communist. Traditionally the difference between them is vast. So let's break them down and see.

The Basic Definition of – LEFTISM:

This term basically refers to those "favouring radical, reforming, or socialist views." A leftist refers to the individual whose political views or policies are of the left.

A person belonging to the political left and usually identifying with the radical, anti capitalist, or revolutionary sectors of left politics. Includes anarchists, Marxists, communists, socialists, and all other explicitly radical left ideologies.[2]

The Basic Definition of – LIBERALISM:

Classical Liberalism: A political philosophy perpetuating free-market economics, minimalist government, strong private property rights, non-interventionism, Government dis-involvement in social issues, separation of church and state, and open borders.

The word "liberal" was originally associated with these beliefs, **but liberals eventually started promoting large government, closed markets, redistribution of wealth, and high government involvement in social issues.** Today, liberal is associated with the latter qualities.

The Newer Liberals: Are sometimes identified as neo-liberals. In modern day, a classical liberal tends to self-identify as a libertarian, and the term classical liberal is used much less than it was 100-200 years ago.[3]

The Basic Definition of a – LIBERAL:

Classically being "liberal" referred to everything that enhanced the freedoms of the "individual," especially freedom from any forms of bondage to: **authoritarianism,** orthodoxy or traditional forms. AND traditionally being liberal meant that you were a person who was willing to respect/accept/tolerate the behaviour or opinions of others that were different from your own. This meant being open to new ideas, which seems to have died today!

Although not all liberals are created equally, liberals used to be tolerant. For example, one day someone said to me: *"I disagree with your views - and most of what you've just said to me,*

BUT I would still 'defend-to-the-death' your right to say it." What a concept! Freedom of speech was still sacred at that point. Not so much today. A modern liberal is a different animal altogether, *(which seems to have lost its way).*

However in its purest form, liberalism was a philosophy that emphasized on **the autonomy of the individual.** Respecting the rights and freedoms of the individual, especially protection for their political and *"civil liberties."* With strong emphasis placed on *"intellectual liberty"* and on *"progress"* and the *"essential goodness of the human race."*

Economically, liberalism was a philosophy that emphasized on free competition, a self-regulating market, and the gold standard. It considered government as a crucial instrument, strictly for betterment of social inequities *(like race, gender and class etc.)* Sounds noble enough? However, like much all else in this politically charged climate, newer liberals have been radicalised.

The Basic Definition of – SOCIALISM:

According to the Merriam Webster Dictionary definition, socialism is defined as: Any of various economic and political theories advocating collective or governmental ownership and administration of the means of production and distribution of goods. A system of society or group living in which there is no private property.

It is a system or condition of society in which the means of production are owned and controlled by the state and considered a *"stage of society"* in Marxist theory, transitional between capitalism and communism and distinguished by unequal distribution of goods and pay according to work done. BUT basically this is saying that socialism is the road to communism.[4]

The Basic Definition of – COMMUNISM:

The theory of Communism may be summed up in one sentence: Abolish all private property.
— Karl Marx[5]

The most basic definition of Communism is in its name. The Latin word *"communis"* literally means *"common, universal."* It is a philosophical, social, political, economic ideology and movement whose ultimate goal is the establishment of a communist society, namely a socioeconomic order structured upon the ideas of common ownership of the means of production and the absence of social classes, money and the state.[6]

Communism is something that, in theory, is a good idea. Communism is an ideal that believes that everyone should share everything, so that **poverty wouldn't exist,** and there wouldn't be a gap between richer and poorer classes. The problem is, **communist governments become corrupt,** because people are greedy, so it doesn't work.[7]

Communism is Revolutionary Socialism:

As I've already said, socialism is the road to communism. AND at times you'll hear communism referred to as *"revolutionary socialism."* However, communism originated as a reaction to the *Industrial Revolution,* and came to be defined by Marx's theories — taken to their extreme end.

This is like saying that the cure is worse than the problem. Many times human nature, when feeling oppressed by the system, will seek change and reform. But in the process of solving one problem, create another much worse. Many bad things have been done in history – but with the best intentions!

Again, Marxists refer to socialism as the first and necessary phase on the way from capitalism to communism *(like riding the wave of both extremes!)* Apparently Marx and Engels themselves didn't consistently or clearly differentiate communism from socialism, which helped ensure lasting confusion between the two terms. BUT again, I will argue, they are essentially the same.[8]

The History & Difference Between Socialism & Communism:

Communism: Under communism, there is no such thing as private property *(yikes, I like my own pair of shoes at least!)* All property is communally owned, and each person receives a portion based on what they need. A strong central government — the state — controls all aspects of economic production, and provides citizens with their basic necessities, including food, housing, medical care and education.

Socialism: By contrast, under socialism, individuals can still own property, *(phew - what a relief. But hang on; if socialism is the road to communism, my shoes are still in danger!)* But industrial production, or the chief means of generating wealth, is communally owned and managed by a democratically elected government.

Socialism is a Less Rigid & More Flexible Ideology Than Communism:

According to Sarah Pruitt, another key difference between socialism and communism is the means of achieving them. In communism, a violent revolution in which the workers rise up against the middle and upper classes is seen as an inevitable part of achieving a pure communist state. Its adherents seek change and reform, but insist on making these changes through democratic processes within the existing social and political structure, not overthrowing that structure.

Socialism and Communism in Practice:

Led by Vladimir Lenin, the Bolsheviks put Marxist theory into practice with the Russian Revolution of 1917, which led to the creation of the world's first communist government. Communism existed in the Soviet Union until its fall in 1991.

A Purely Communist State has Never Existed:

Today, communism exists in China, Cuba, North Korea, Laos and Vietnam — although in reality, a purely communist state has never existed. Such countries can be classified as communist because in all of them, the central government controls all aspects of the economic and political system. But none of them have achieved the elimination of personal property, money or class systems that the communist ideology requires.

A Purely Socialist State has Never Existed:

Likewise, no country in history has achieved a state of pure socialism. Even countries that are considered by some people to be socialist states, like **Norway, Sweden and Denmark, have successful capitalist sectors** and follow policies that are largely aligned with social democracy. Many European and Latin American countries have adopted socialist programs *(such as free college tuition, universal health care and subsidized child care)* and even elected socialist leaders, with varying levels of success.

The Growing Movement of - Democratic Socialism:

Pruitt says that in the United States, socialism has not historically enjoyed as much success as a political movement. Its peak came in 1912, when Socialist Party presidential candidate Eugene V. Debs won 6 percent of the vote. But at the same time, U.S. programs once considered socialist, such as Medicare and Social Security, have been integrated into American life.

Democratic socialism - a growing U.S. political movement in recent years - lands somewhere in between social democracy and communism.

Like communists, democratic socialists believe workers should control the bulk of the means of production, and not be subjected to the will of the free market and the capitalist classes. **But they believe their vision of socialism must be achieved through democratic processes, rather than revolution** *(but this is arguable, going by the behaviour of some).*[9]

ENDNOTES:

1. https://www.urbandictionary.com/define.php?term=antifa

2. https://www.urbandictionary.com/define.php?term=Leftist

3. https://www.urbandictionary.com/define.php?term=classical%20liberalism

4. https://www.merriam-webster.com/dictionary/socialism

5. https://www.urbandictionary.com/define.php?term=Communism

6. https://en.wikipedia.org/wiki/Communism

7. https://www.urbandictionary.com/define.php?term=Communism

8. https://www.history.com/news/socialism-communism-differences

9. https://www.history.com/news/socialism-communism-differences; Sarah Pruitt

10. Excerpts of this chapter taken from "Coronavirus - Communist and Marxist Uprising" by Dr Alan Pateman, Copyright © 2020, Published by APMI Publications

❖

Ministry Profile

Dr Alan is Founder and President, CEO of **Alan Pateman Ministries International** (APMI), with his international Head Office located in Italy *(overseeing national offices in different locations)*, and which umbrellas the following divisions:

The first is "Connecting for Excellence" (CFE) apostolic network, which is a multi-facetted missions organisation with the purpose of connecting leaders for divine opportunities and building lasting relationships. Apostle Alan has to date ordained more than 500 ministers in over 50 nations. In addition there are ministries, churches and schools who are in Association or Affiliation, looking to him to provide spiritual oversight, personal mentorship and accountability.

Yearly conferences are being hosted *(where possible)* in different locations, to provide support and encouragement.

Secondly, *(the teaching arm or division)* **"LifeStyle International Christian University"** (LICU), founded in 2007, is a study program for students who desire to invest time from their lives into university studies where they can receive from the Anointed Word of God; not only to receive academic credits but an impartation that brings personal transformation. The same program can be applied for correspondence studies including identical syllabuses and study material designed for distance learning. Resulting in the same certification at the end of their studies! Degrees offered range from, a "Diploma in Theology" to a "Doctor of Philosophy" for those who decide to go through the full university program.

LICU is a global network, operating from different nations *(overseeing correspondence students and regional campuses)*, with a board of executive directors, professors, national directors, faculty members and administrational staff. The national directors and teams work with the International Oversight and Head Office, located in Italy. Our purpose is to demonstrate the Supernatural Kingdom of God through Doctrinal, Apostolic and Prophetic Teaching.

Graduation ceremonies are held every year in different nations, such as Cameroon, the Netherlands, Italy, UK and so on.

- LifeStyle International Christian University - Dr Alan holds the position of President, CEO, Professor of Theology, Biblical Studies and Apostolic Ministry *(currently LICU is exploding throughout Europe, Asia and Africa)*

- Note: *There is also the International Apostolic Accreditation Council (a network of Christian professional educators, bible schools, leadership forums and university programs to provide both credibility through association and credibility through accountability)*

The third division is APMI Publishing and Publications: we are committed to providing authors with an affordable and easy way to publish their manuscripts. Enabling them to share their books with millions of readers by making it available as paperback, hardcover and/or eBook copies on international outlets such as Amazon, iBookStore, Nook Store, Kobo Store, Walmart, Bol, Rakute, Google, Allegro, and other big platforms.

Dr Alan is known as an accomplished author and prolific writer, who has published over eighty books *(to date)* and teaching materials, *(that have been made available in most formats)*. For example, his popular online **"Letters to the Church"** called, Truth for the Journey, has developed a worldwide audience, including the latest venture, **Watchers of the 4 kings.**

On a personal note, Alan the family man, who grew up on an English farm, still enjoys long walks in the countryside with his family today. Still an avid walker, he spends many hours in the Tuscan hills and beautiful coastlines! Beyond his primary passions *(family and Christ)*, Alan has a very creative eye and innovative flare. As a talented artist, Alan loves painting large modern abstract canvases, but all forms of art and design are always stimulating to him, especially architecture and interior design. Not excluding the fact that Alan has always designed his own media materials, book covers and websites etc.

However, no matter how busy life gets, Dr Alan and his wife Jenny appreciate being surrounded by family and friends, children and growing number of grandchildren. They reside in Barga, Tuscany *(The Eagle's Nest*)*, Italy.

Alan Pateman Ph.D., D.Min., D.D., M.A., B.Th.

ENDNOTES:

1. *The Eagle's Nest is a prophetic vision that God gave to Alan in 1996. He said, "Italy is your Nest *(Ministry International Head-Office)* and from it you will fly out, to and fro, to the nations."

2. Dr. Alan Pateman attended several colleges throughout his training *(including studying Theology at Roffey Place, Horsham, UK and a Member of Kerygma - with Rev. Colin Urquhart and Dr. Bob Gordon - 1985-1987)*

before being awarded a Doctorate of Divinity *(2006)* in recognition of his lifetime achievements by the International College of Excellence, now "DanEl Christian College" *(President: Dr. Robb Thompson USA)* also "Life Christian University" *(Dr. Douglas Wingate USA)* where he also earned a Bachelor of Theology B.Th. *(2006)*, a Master of Arts in Theology M.A., a Doctor of Ministry in Theology D.Min., *(2007)* and Doctor of Philosophy in Theology Ph.D. *(2013)* from LICU.

❖

To Contact the Author

Please email:

Alan Pateman Ministries International

Email: apostledr@alanpateman.com
Web: www.AlanPatemanMinistries.com

*Please include your prayer requests
and comments when you write.*

❖

Other Books

China, Covid-19, World Domination

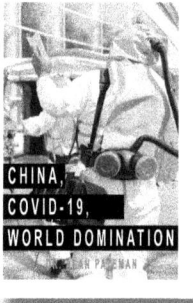

Church, this period is a wake up call. The world uses the term "woke" to describe this. The church must be "woke," but not to the propaganda and deception of this world, but to the truth of what God wants to do in the earth today.

ISBN: 978-1-909132-85-6, Pages: 132,
Format: Paperback, Published: 2020
Also available in eBook format!

Watchers of the 4 kings

China represents a military superpower that fears no other nation on earth. Described as the "East" or "sun rising" in the bible, we know this refers to China. This particular king is predicted to lead a mammoth army that will march in numbers exceeding 200 million soldiers, as described in scripture *(Daniel 7).*

ISBN: 978-1-909132-87-0, Pages: 120,
Format: Paperback, Published: 2020
Also available in eBook format!

Truth for the Journey Books

Coronavirus – Communist and Marxist Uprising

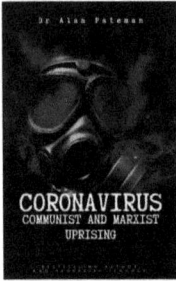

Within this book Dr Pateman analyses the current world events, providing definitions of terminologies that are easily confused; and exposes the reality that China's real disease is NOT Covid-19 but indeed "COMMUNISM."

ISBN: 978-1-909132-89-4, Pages: 112,
Format: Paperback, Published: 2020
Also available in eBook format!

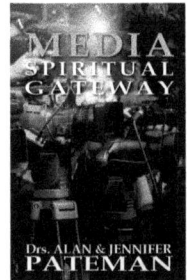

Media, Spiritual Gateway

Let's face it; we live in the era of fake news! It's always existed, but never been quite so prominent. Today it's an all-out-war between fact and political fiction. The media has been sabotaged by political activism. Gone are the days of impartiality and objective unbiased reporting, with many sources saying that true journalism is dead.

ISBN: 978-1-909132-54-2, Pages: 192,
Format: Paperback, Published: 2018
Also available in eBook format!

LIFESTYLE
UNIVERSITY

Raising Up
Christian Leaders

Dear Friends,

Have you considered becoming one of our international students? We are privileged to welcome you, from around the world, to "LifeStyle International Christian University" *(the teaching arm of Alan Pateman Ministries International)*. **An English speaking university** dedicated to your success; to see you trained and equipped to fully succeed in your God given Destiny.

It is our passion to raise up the leaders of tomorrow, who will have influence in all realms of authority, including the Body of Christ. Men and women of strategy, wisdom and true godliness, who'll stand with stature and maturity in this hour.

It's undeniable that in today's world, recognised education has become indispensable, therefore it is our desire to offer well balanced and well structured courses. Those that have been written by gifted and talented ministers of God, who seek to be inspired by God's Holy Spirit.

Consequently we have put together a **flexible curriculum,** designed both for correspondence students and campuses, which is a strategy to reach the distant learner; whether provincial, national or international. In fact we have many correspondence students from around the world, including a growing number of successful campuses, in various countries.

This is a growing platform, where men and women of dignity and passion, can grow and be established in their God given endeavours. As God is the healer of the nations, we pray and believe that many of our alumni will go on to **become world changers** in their own right.

We are proud of each and every one of our LICU students.
It would be our pleasure if you would join them on this incredible journey!

Doctor Alan Pateman

Alan Pateman Prof. Ph.D., D.Min., D.D., M.A., B.Th.
PRESIDENT AND CEO
www.licuuniversity.com   www.cfeapostolicnetwork.com
Email: info@licuuniversity.com   Mob: +39 366 329 1315

For more information visit our website/facebook or contact our office, using the details below:

Website: www.licuuniversity.com
Facebook: www.facebook.com/LICUMainCampus
Email: info@licuuniversity.com
Telephone: +39 366 329 1315